Your Thoughts CREATE You

ISBN: 1-4679-3680-4
ISBN-13: 9781467936804

Your Thoughts CREATE You

And the % of LIGHT you CARRY

Bonnie Baumgartner

CONTENTS

My website is www.mysticknowing.com
    On line dictionary and articles are available

Acknowledgments

Teachers LEARN by teaching and teach by LIS-TENING. My gratitude goes to all those with and without biology that have trusted my listening skills. Thank you to all the humans that have helped me with their thoughts, awareness, and energy. Their soul aspects have been gracious in all the information they share. THANK YOU

Dan Laudicina who is living and sharing his en-trainments with me. His soul aspect gives a different point of perception than mine and fills in aware-ness I miss and examples I can use.

Torben Hansen that shares his knowledge, balance and little human patterns to release. He comes from the higher mental plane often. http://www.look4insight.com   http://aware-nesshealsme.com

Kelly Arbogast communes with his soul aspects creatively and knows things. He created and serves as the Webmaster on the Mystic Knowing website. http://www.mysticknowing.com

Suzanne Lie http://www.suzanneliephd.com
Brice Taylor wrote THANKS for the MEMORIES
Judith Spencer wrote SATAN''S High Priest
Michael Lewis wrote BOOMERANG, 2011.

Introduction

YOUR THOUGHTS CREATE YOU
And the % of LIGHT you CARRY

The chaos and changes happening all around us can be viewed as constructive restructuring of the way we have thought and functioned historically. The increased light and vibration from the sun and photon belt are waking people up. They are questioning if the way they have always functioned is the best way to go. Those not wanting to awaken are experiencing more pain and suffering and acting out because the old unethical, secretive and illegal activity is being exposed and there are consequences.

The process of awakening spiritually is a radically different experience than what we have experienced before. Most of what we consider FACTS of our reality and universe are not accurate. The perceptions of our realities are fragile, temporary ever changing constructs. We are being called to action and to start thinking for our self. We need to move from considering our self a victim or "the crazy person" to a conscious creator that has compassion for the self first.

A constructive plan of action is easy when there is nothing hidden and no hidden agendas to second-guess at. In the higher vibrations there is no denial or secrets or dissociation from the self or others. The cruel thoughtless things we do are not pretty or nice they are darkness feeding off darkness. We covered up OUR awareness of our dark thoughts because we didn't like or approve of them. What you created individually and as a group you need to uncreate individually and as a group. The wisdom comes when you KNOW why you created what you have and the tweaks and adjusting needed to create more compassion and equality for you and others.

The information in my books is my way of sharing my perception of the larger picture. Possibly that will help you on your path of awareness.

Chapter 1
ENERGY FOLLOWS THOUGHT

Your thoughts define you and the light you carry. The universe is made up of quantum energy or light particles. The percentage of light particles you emanate is based on the type of thoughts you dwell in. Each thought has a particular vibration and sound just as a bell does. Lower sounds and vibrational thoughts like worry, upset and complaining carry less quantum energy or light.

The universal principle of **THOUGHT** is that energy follows your THOUGHT. Seek or wonder about something and your thought will take you there. You need to discern what is true or valuable for you in what you find.

The universal principle of **VIBRATION** is that everything in the universe, physical or NOT moves in waves or circular patterns and has a unique vibration, color and sound. That applies to all our sensory perceptions, feelings and thoughts.

The human BRAIN is the processing center used to keep the biology alive in this LIFETIME. The mind or mental body found in our aura and our biology use the brain to communicate with each other. The right hemisphere of the brain represents our spiritual side and infinity. The left hemisphere of the brain allows us to pretend to be a human and have a past, present and future in this reality or matrix or dimension. The two hemispheres are being reconnected so we will have awareness of our spirituality and infinity. The synaptic pathways are being rewired into loops instead of strands. We are also developing a third strand of RNA/DNA to handle our expansion.

The universal principle of **PROJECTION** is that you created your STORY with your thoughts. Your reality is YOU projecting your thoughts into this reality or matrix or dimension. Any reality is constructed by agreement with all parties involved to determine the controlling matrix or grid system in a given reality. Reality is a complex concept with many never-ending definitions. Your stories can only be changed or rewritten from within you by changing your thoughts in the now moment. Those wishing to see joyful experiences instead of reruns, trash, and violence must refuse to allow such things to fill them.

The principle of **AWARENESS** is that you NEED to observe the illusion of separation that duality presents and realizes how many dark truths there are on earth. This reality is a role-playing game designed to increase your discernment and spiritual wisdom about the way dark behaves and the truths the dark hold and live by.

Most of us have been operating with the "dark rules of survival" and staying alive. We have been raised, taught, used and controlled by dark truths. Religion and darkness have been dismal failures at teaching people to love and create for themselves. When you don't have compassion for you FIRST your ability to love anything or anyone else is drastically reduced. Ascension is out of the question when you fail to love yourself first.

Historically our negative beliefs have locked us into giving away our power to the biggest bully and their dark agendas that cycle is over. Have faith that we can be compassionate with each other as our old reality is collapsing and new points of perception are being adopted. We are being inundated with higher vibrations of energy especially around October 28th, 2011 and December 21 2012. The new light reflects and supports the new reality we are creating.

We have three energy fields that are considered a part of our BODY. There is the biology and out from that is our emotional body or aura where all our unresolved traumas and experiences are there for all to see. Each thought you have is an individual entity that has an image, vibration, color, shape and movement. Gaia's emotional body is the 4th dimension that surrounds her physical body the earth. Then comes our MIND or MENTAL BODY that surrounds the emotional body. For Gaia the mental body is the 5th dimension that carries unity, peace and compassion. The intuition and sensory perceptions the human gets is from their mental body not the brain. Knowingness comes from the mental body and is instantaneous. The mental body can sense or know in advance when a synchronicity is about to happen. The brain won't know about it until after it happens. Then the brain will process what took place, file and categorize what happened. Around and through the center of our biology and Gaia's is the spiritual body.

The 6th dimension for humans and Gaia is creativity, planning and reworking our alignment with universal law. Reality or the matrix on earth is BASED on the group thoughts that form this holograph. Our thought patterns, vibrations, sound and light reflect our own personal moral character and behavior and maybe the groups moral character and behavior or maybe not. Most, around 60 to 70% of earth's population is rather negative or dark and unconscious. They tend to dwell in thoughts of self-hate or numb dissociation. The unconscious consider them self to be victims always blaming another and tend to be vengeful, angry, antagonistic, addicted living life in anxiety and fear. That could be the clan you were raised in and if it was than you were also used and abused, but I am sure they called it LOVE and you were lucky to get it. Then YOU had a family and continued the tradition or not?

All forms of mental domination or brainwashing can only work when there is FEAR present. Compassion for the self creates a sense of equality and self-worth that prevents the fear and doubt needed to control a person. The dark and unconscious are bullies that use and abuse other humans and especially children and animals because they are too small to fight back or demand humane treatment. They are deeply wounded people with no compassion for what they suffered as children. They are easily possessed by any dark entity and the most likely possession is a dark ancestor. To deal with their suffering they shut off their feelings and senses. The purpose of rituals is to have all members intensely focus on a single thought and image to push a particular agenda even if it is "peace and love" goes against the law of allowing.

The universal law of **ALLOWING** means releasing attachment to YOUR need for others to be the way you want them to be. Stop trying to please or change others and release your judgment, blame and attachment to what the dark ones want you to do, say, be or think. Allowing grants to all the same rights you want for yourself. The right to have, be and do whatever you choose as long as you avoid violating others rights or destroying our collective environment.

THOUGHT EMANATES LIGHT

Several soul aspects work closely with the human at all times. You may or may not be consciously aware of their presence. A large percentage of the time they communicate through our sensory perceptions. That is your gut feeling and your knowingness that something is going to happen before it does. When you hear your voice in YOUR head that is your soul aspect communicating. Your soul aspects unlike most humans have retained their knowledge about your personal history and con-current experiences and life on other dimensions. They are aware of all entities you have ever inter-acted with.

The agreed upon rules of the earth reality is that the soul aspects are to help and support the human. When the little human lowers their vibration as a result making many dark choices the soul as-pects get pressured into following the little human into the lower vibrational bands and thought pat-terns making both a darker gray. The little human can drag the soul aspects into increasing darkness. When the human wants to go BLACK the soul as-pects will abandon the biology and that has hap-pened to 15% of the population on Gaia.

The soul aspects, just like the biology or human a soul aspect inhabits, gets traumatized by the vio-lent experiences the little human has on Gaia. The abuse, force and negativity we visit on each other is more than our soul aspects can process leaving the soul aspects confused, ignorant and dark. This can be true for a long time and for many lifetimes. Especially the abuses parents intentionally com-mit on their children. When soul aspects follow the human into dark thought patterns they may well pass along their dark negative thought and mes-sages to the little human. For example when the human asks the soul "What do you think of me?" and the response is negative or belittling that is a soul aspect that is confused, ignorant and gone dark. Only a dark soul aspect will tell you that you are stupid, ugly, and evil, not worthy or encourage the human in abusive behaviors. You can ask for a 100% light aspect to answer your questions. A soul aspect that carries light is always honest but never negative. Any answers you get that are negative, dark or confusing ignore.

The vibrational band or dark the human has chosen for it self or "the reality it has created" with its thought patterns triggers the law of attraction to bring on more of the same. Universal law of attraction brings you more of what you created with your thoughts. You get IMMERSION THERAPY to see if that is what you really want all the time. Your soul aspects will keep lining up synchronicities for you in your vibrational thought patterns. If you enjoy worrying, blaming, judging or forcing you will get even more of that. There is no super hero or magic that will get you OUT of a particular vibrational band. The human, thought itself into that vibration and you need to THINK your way to a different vibration and bring your dark soul aspects with you. It is your job to change their thought.

Dark thoughts and the resulting behavior might have started a great many life times ago for the little human. There is many dark soul-to-soul agreements or entrainments made with other dark human souls we are still honoring. These agreements trigger the universal law of entrainment to hold you in a band of darkness all together. Humans have had MANY dark lifetimes of codependency or being the victim and predator. Fear breeds the need to control and have power continuing the cycle that recreates itself all the time. Universal law SUPPORTS what you create with your thought with the law of attraction and entrainment they give you more of what you have UNTIL your thinking changes. Universal attraction does not care if your emanations are real or IMAGINED, negative or positive. When a human holds the frequency of war, vengeance, anger or hate that becomes the frequency you emanate and attract to yourself.

When you ADOPT the belief or obsession another created and you dwell in it that becomes your truth and what you emanate. When you emanate or project a vibration of fear you are NOT FORCED to do anything. You have become the CREATOR or catalyst for anger, vengeance and violence. When you emanate victimhood, trickery or self-hate a family member has introduced you to and you dwell in those thoughts you have adopted them as your own. When you are suffering it is because your thought is misdirected, ignorant or confused. Collect new information to create a larger, positive picture for yourself. You need to rescue you by having higher vibrational thought and following universal laws.

Some of earth's population is HALF CONSCIOUS as they go in and out of awareness. They function in fear, indifference or boredom. They operate by being oppositional, angry or in pain. They are self-absorbed, dramatic, gossip and frequently leave their biology to live in past time. They are limited by their fears and irrational beliefs. They twist facts to defend their reality. The half conscious believe they are better than you so they can force you to do things their way. They blame you and gossip about you to make you feel worthless and keep you in your place. Adults give this negative feedback to children. Blame allows you to AVOID taking responsibility for YOU and what you think.

In half conscious families, religion, businesses and national beliefs fear of pain or punishment is the motivator. They allow bullies and leaders to do their thinking for them surrendering their personal thought and freedom. When you stop thinking for yourself you are powerless, robotic and predictable as most humans are. The vast majority of our society is unconsciously programmed to fit in and not make waves. Venting or leaving your trance or dissociated state long enough to express rage or anger is not thinking that is reacting.

Prayer, mantras or saying your rosary is giving your power away and asking another to do what you need to do consciously for the self. A good soldier or follower needs a good leader. Being the follower or leader goes against universal law. Each of us must create and focus on our own thoughts, awareness and reality. Control and saving others is you trying to force your reality on others. That helps none and keeps you in a low vibration.

The half conscious, more light than dark human with over 50% light emanates some grayish light because there is always a hidden agenda with their light so it is not pure. They are able to consciously create some.

Those that are ¾ light or conscious are conventional, traditional, cautious, hopeful and upset themselves when others do not follow the rules. They tend to squelch enthusiasm and inventiveness in others. They are followers and want to fit in. They like to be entertained. They start showing compassion for the SELF and can tap into the "universal sources of information" them self without an entity as a go between like a guide, angel, ascended master, alien or your higher self. There are no secrets in lighter vibrations. Everyone has access to everything all information. You are aware that you have never been a victim and created victim experiences to increase your depth of understanding the dark or unconsciousness. The dark presents endless moral dilemmas to mold, develop and create our moral character and choices. The legion of light imposed quarantine on earth roughly 12,500 years ago when Atlantis sank and the earth plunged into darkness. We have experienced frustration, misery and pain to let us know we needed to make different choices.

MORE LIGHT than DARK

You are the one that can make you joyful. You are the one that needs to be compassionate with you. You are the one doing the spiritual work with your other soul aspects. A great deal is possible when you have the discipline, skill set, focus and compassion to carry out and manifest. It takes work to leave dark and unconsciousness. Incomplete thought, sloppy and self-deceptive illusion and no structure is not light. Darkness is not really interested in the discipline needed to carry through a plan and stay with it to completion. When you are going lighter and those close to you are staying darker can you release your attachment to them? CAN you honor the direction they choose and stay on your path? Going light takes different skills than remaining dark. You need to realize which skills are actually used in the light and what skills and truths are dark.

The Law of allowing is on a continuum from murder, force or total control to picking up your companion animal and squeezing it when it does not want to be held. Where do you fall most of the time on the continuum of allowing? What are you attached too. What are you failing to do for you?

There is great reverence for light soul contracts in the universe. The contracts made with darkness are frequently broken and should not be followed when they are against you caring for you. Sacrifice and self-sacrifice is a dark concept and against universal law. When a relationship or contract goes stagnant it has ended but humans are very attached to breathing life into the dead and trying to force others to conform to their reality. The more you get attached to a thing, person or event the more you abandon yourself and worship something or someone else. The more attached you are the darker you go and the less you value yourself. Valuing another individual, thing or belief over the self is dark truth.

The more you value another the greater is the burden you put on them and the greater your suffering is when it is lost or fails you. Attachment to belittling others or forcing a child to care for you emotionally always results in suffering and increased karma for the parties involved. Self-love is you caring for YOU and honoring your needs physically, emotionally and spiritually, first. We can only give to others what we give ourselves first.

Our biology is a vehicle and learning tool used to have dark experiences by the many little choices we make as we gave away our energy to others and leaders and stopped thinking for ourselves. As we got increasingly darker we attached to what would keep our biology alive. We became physically and emotionally attached to stuff or people that could keep the biology safe and satisfied. Most behaviors in the "earth illusion" are about maintaining the biology physically.

Those that are fully conscious do not let an entity or demon posses them and they do not dissociate abandoning the biology. They are light enough for the soul aspect to enter the space around your biology your aura and "the little human" starts to merge with their soul aspect. They have had their half dark / half light ascension. They are joyful and enthusiastic. They have committed to being compassionate with them self and their biology. Their guides, angels, higher self and imaginary friends say good-by one way or another but you need to notice them leave. You will feel lonely but you are NOT abandoned. You are not being upgraded. The old falls apart and there is a time lag until the new kicks in or gets down loaded. You need faith during the time lag or zero point energy as you are in the void. Grieve for what you were and what you experienced. Zero-point energy is universal energy at rest or the lowest level of activity. Your first awareness may feel like being stuck because motion has stopped and is balanced or neutral.

The VOID or EMPTY feeling or portal is what we go through when what has been usual and customary for us ends. There is empty aloneness. A void happens after you realize a belief you always operated with is no longer a truth for you. You need to release the old truths before adopting new truths. When your beliefs crumble there is grieving, HURT, pain and JOY that can be experienced during this process. Grieve the changes and any lose you might feel. Cut the cords to relationships no longer serving you. Give back any darkness you have carried for others as a child and especially from family members. Now you can rewrite your concurrent lifetimes. New thoughts will come into your awareness as mental and emotional processing and transmuting go on. Generally voids last a few months or weeks. We go into the void many times this is not a one-time event.

The movement from functioning as a little human in survival mode to stay alive on a dark planet takes developing some serious dark skills. It has been survival of the fittest or the smartest one wins or the biggest bully wins. Staying alive is the contest of "when I win, you lose." The skills we learned from the family and mastered to survive are dark and frequently the opposite of what is needed to live by universal law.

Realize that what you THINK to yourself and the emotion you FEEL vibrate as loud and strong as anything you have ever said aloud. The judgments in your head are being felt. Secrets are gone now you are becoming transparent. Lies, withholds, denial will create a distance between your soul aspect and you. Your soul aspect will wait until you SEE the bits of darkness or density left in you. You will get the same awareness over and over dressed up in different ways. Learning to allow is a hard lesson. The more you go against the law of allowing the darker your energy balance goes and the further away you push your soul. There is no one to rescue or save or enlighten but you. When others ask for information or guidance and you discern they will understand what you offer share.

Some are working on ASCENDING as Gaia is and then you function more with your soul aspects than you do with the ego or little human. 2% of the population on earth has had at least "one LIGHT ascension" when you consider all their lifetimes on earth. We need to show gratitude to our biology for all its service to us. The biology is transforming from carbon base to crystalline base. Our immune system has worked by fighting invaders now the THYMUS absorbs and transmute invaders. Our chakras are activating and growing in number.

All vibrations of our reality are present in the now moment. We choose to think about, visit or dwell in the 3rd, 4th, 5th or 6th dimension by giving it our attention. The thoughts you have during your different life experiences places you into a particular vibration or dimension for a long or short space of time that is always in your control.

Some solid 3rd dimension vibrations are you being upset or constantly vigilant, which is YOUR fear or you creating drama, being violent or bored or being sexually addicted. In the 3rd dimension the little human rules the soul and forces the biology.

Fun, creativity and laughter are mostly middle 4th dimensional.

Peaceful, compassionate and unconditional love are 5th dimensional.

Seeing the big picture, reworking what hasn't worked, understanding higher vibrational cause and affect and alignment with universal law, as the conscious creator you are is 6th dimensional abilities. Monitoring and controlling your thoughts get you to the 6th dimensional vibration.

The activities, individuals, places or things you experience evoke THOUGHTS and feelings in you.

Our feelings have different vibrations that belong to one dimension or another. The feeling or vibration you are in most of the time is the reality you choose to perceive. In an instant you can change dimensions. You can wakeup in the peaceful 5th dimension and upset yourself about most anything to go right into the 3rd dimension. Fear, anger or addictions taking center stage will hold you in 3rd dimensional vibrations. What you calibrate your consciousness and attention to will be your reality because you triggered the law of attraction to bring you MORE of what you have so you can SEE externally what is going on in your thoughts internally.

Pretty stories, denial, dissociation and complaining calibrate you into 3rd dimensional vibrations. Anything or anyone vibrating lower than the 5th dimension is earth-bound. Any attachment you have to the earth bound will diminish your ability to stay in the 5th dimension.

Gaia, the photon belt and our sun are raising their vibration and consequently your vibration. You will not be held in the 5th dimension when you choose 3rd dimension thinking and thought patterns for your focus and reality. ATTENDING to things in your reality like suffering humans, animals and plants lowers your vibration trapping you into the 3rd dimensional vibration. Putting your focus and energy into endeavors that you CANNOT help or change and go against the law of allowing will greatly lower your resonance. Extinct plants and animals have moved up in vibration and are alive and well in the 5th dimension. Your "suffering lovers," relatives, friends and "the masses" (YOUR perception is that they are suffering) are creating and focusing on their reality and you need to allow that or enjoy staying in the 3rd dimension to give them YOUR conditional love or caretaking to make YOU feel important, special and in control of their reality.

Chapter 2
PHYSICAL TRAPS

Earth is unique in that it represents all the different types of life found throughout the Milky Way Galaxy with its large variety of animals, plants and minerals. Gaia is unique because she is accomplishing the shift into higher dimensions in a very short time. In the past it took many lifetimes of preparation for the biology and spiritual wisdom to be integrated enough to ascend. Those vibrating with less light are going to be relocated to a 4th dimensional reality because they chose to learn more from duality and how dark functions.

Owning MORE STUFF or forcing people is one of the many physical traps that will bind you to lower vibrations. Thinking your value is based on what you own or control outside of you is also low vibration. Release YOUR attachment to things and people that have chosen to hold onto the lower vibration. We have operated with the "dark rules of survival" and staying alive for more than the last 12 thousand years. Each generation has been raised by and taught how to use and control with dark truths. Religion and darkness have double standards and lots of secrets. None of our teachings have been about self-compassion. You can only successfully work with others AFTER you have mastered working with you. Otherwise your focus on them instead of being compassion for you means you will join them in their darker imbalance. Both of you will be giving your energy to the immediate "little human WOUND" and you will fail to notice the universal laws you are ignoring. Your focus on those that are unconscious and choose dark is YOU forcing your reality on them.

If you want to align with universal law, you can "hold a space" for them. Holding a space is being aware of when another person asks for support or information and is vibrating high enough to embrace what you share with them. When their focus continues to be on their immediate WOUND instead of the spiritual wisdom to be gained "by them" you wait. You hold a space without being controlling, manipulative, worried, guilty, or focusing on the other person. You WAIT for them to get clarity on the bigger spiritual picture or lesson they CHOSE to be in the middle of at this time.

The universal principle of **LIABILITY** says we are held liable for the use, abuse or neglect of the rights we have and earned.

The planets and stars in this quadrant of our universe are all ascending now. The various populations on the planets will need to raise their vibration or be relocated. For example the Bellatricians migrated from the Constellation of Sagittarius about 25 million years ago. For the past six million years they and the Anunnaki have acted as chief administrators for the Draco Empire for this sector of the

Milky Way Galaxy including earth. They were former members of the Anchara Alliance or League of Orion. In 1995 they signed the Treaty of Anchara ending the war between the dark and light and the GROUP agreed to move to greater light. Some individuals and small groups are holding the lower vibrations. The Bellatrician group became members of the Galactic Federation around 2005. The Bellatricians are a dinosaur / reptilian hybrid and are moving as a group from 3rd dimension to higher dimensions as the earth is.

The Agarthans live in the Inner or Hallow earth with Gaia's blessing. After Lemuria fell 13 thousand years ago some refugees from Lemuria and Atlantis settled inside the earth. Their environment conforms to the people's wants and creativity. Agarthans function in the 5th dimension BUT 15% of them are dark and will be relocated. There is a billion of the Agarthans acting as mentors to those of us on the surface overseeing the earth and its shift. You need to discern if their thought patterns resonate with your thoughts as you work with them.

Other aliens and extraterrestrials assisting us are the Andromedans, Pleiadians, Arcturians and other members of the Galactic Federation. The Andromedans come from the Andromeda Galaxy, a spiral galaxy twice the size of our galaxy located 2 million light years away. The ANDROMEDAN COUNCIL has 139 different races represented on it to facilitate the evolution of all civilizations in the Milky Way Galaxy by mentoring them. They facilitate innovative strategies for resolving conflict and making decisions with the Galactic community in dealing with the situation on earth. The council helps educate and work to fill in the information we lack about our history. The council considers the earth population as self-destructive and abusive to each other a learned dark behavior pattern. Our politics and religions are self-serving creating drama, war, and fear. They are exposing the elite's manipulation of people and improving global governance diplomacy and conflict resolution.

Andromedans are considered healers of the body, mind, emotions and spirit. They have intervened in the ancient past to help resolve very serious conflicts in this part of the universe. They teach how to integrate belief systems and emotions to create harmony and balance. Andromedans are helping the population raise their overall levels of consciousness on earth. They live in 5th dimensional reality. They have no military. Everything that they create technologically is used for the advancement of their race or for educational purposes BUT could be used defensively if needed. There is no financial system because the people are given what they need.

The Pleiadians are humanoid and come from the Pleiades star system. They were originally refugees from the Lyrean civilization. Some of them colonized the Atlantean civilization and they carried 60% light at that time. During the Roman Empire, 27 BC thru 476 on earth the civilization of Pleiadian-Plejarans was around 60% light. They do not use currency. Resources of their planet are shared with all the people. Material goods are freely given based on your contribution to society. They feel politics and religion is the same thing. Just because a group is labeled "Pleiadians" doesn't mean they are here to help us. As a group they are emotionally and spiritually more evolved than we are. As a group they function in 5th dimensional reality and want us to be aware of them and they are pushing for us to wake up and evolve.

Arcturians settled in the constellation of Arcturus and were accepted into the Galactic Federation approximately 3.75 million years ago. They are a horse-like mammalian closely resembling a horse. Their highly developed spiritual nature has allowed them to avoid aging, violence, war, sickness, poverty and pollution. They terminate life when the contract that has been arranged for their existence is finished. They have peaceful ways and do not interfere with others. Arcturians are noted for their mastery of science and philosophy. They are benevolent beings from the 7th dimension and higher. Arcturians are helping us integrate spiritual values with advanced technologies. They provide strategic advice in transforming planetary systems and coordinating relationships with extraterrestrials. They are helping us integrating our global financial, political and societal systems and use diplomacy with conflict resolution. Arcturians have been an integral part of earth's history for eons just as the other civilizations have.

WANTING not ENJOYING

Wanting means YOU are unaware that you already have it and are not enjoying it is one more physical trap. Everything you IMAGINE you create or ALL you remember is REAL. Have you looked in all the corners? You think it and the molecules gather together to create it or point out what you are not seeing. Our thoughts and feelings are filters that influence our perceptions. It is imperative to accept that you are not and never have been a victim. The victim is one that takes no responsibility for their situation or creation and blames others or takes from others. Those behaviors increase their darkness and attachment to matter.

Your emotion and thoughts define you and your continuous creating. FEAR creates the many unpleasant things you have seen and experienced. Fear is almost as powerful a creational force as compassion even though it is NOT REAL to the soul and higher vibrations. In fear we automatically victimize the self and attract more to us. The little human thinks fear is real and it is to the biology. Loss of the biology rather than surrendering to darkness is fine with your soul. Neutralize your fear and heal it with more information and COMPASSION for you first. Fear is the unknown or LACK of information and not the opposite of love. As we walk through our fears and worries we transmute fear into something more useful for us.

Fear WITHHOLDS LOVE from the self. Defensive posture creates disintegration of and drains our spiritual energy and physical strength. When you are having fun it's easier to release old patters of behavior. Creations based in fear are creations of restriction or control that starts in the gut as a lower energy vibration and can be controlled by our thoughts BEFORE it moves into the mind to overwhelm you. Recognize, identify and challenge your fear to prevent it from dictating your actions. Talking to your fear means you OWN it and are embracing it because you let it express itself, you listened. Fear is intense and was designed to HELP US and often has information or clarity we need to discern higher truths. Anger, fear and self-doubt are dark creations. When your thoughts are STUCK in "I don't deserve" "don't want" you strengthen the darkness you wrapped yourself in to protect your self from being wounded one more time.

When we are ready for any change fear comes in to challenge our resolve. When we are filled with compassion for our self the "options of greater light" will be noticed and used.

FREE-FLOATING fear is when you are unable to attach your fear to a current situation it is about an old incident or old pattern of yours frequently from childhood. Fear returns UNTIL you acknowledge the pain and education it gave you. MURDERERS have no compassion for the wounds their childhood or past lives created in them.

Looking from the point of perception of a murderer, there is one of two different reasons for killing others. One type kills out of frustration at their inability to communicate their wants or needs affectively to another in their environment. To end their frustration and express the depth of their need they kill. Maybe they kill the person that is choosing to withhold what they think they need or the victim is incapable of giving the murder what they want. Or maybe they kill someone else that is easier to kill. Then they will vent on an innocent, like joining the military to kill strangers or killing a cat, dog, spouse or smaller child.

The other group is FEARFUL and ANGRY and considers the actual physical death of another the end of the fun, the end of warding off their fear that they might be the next to be tormented and tortured. This group of killers is after the JOY of tormenting their victim and being grateful it isn't them being tortured. Finally THEY are in control. The Illuminati Satanists are included in this group. This entire group of killers, bullies and tormentors has been tormented and bullied as infants and children BUT haven't been killed. When they have an opportunity to torment or attract or create an opportunity to torment they do. They strive for MAXIMUM suffering and fear because they feed off of that energy it makes them feel alive and powerful. They feel if they are doing the torturing they are safe another day from being the victim.

The ones murdering and torturing eventually become less and less satisfied with their adrenaline rush, their fears have not left them and their quality of life sucks. The gray ones in the lower 4th dimension and the murderers still in biology are going darker and their life force is leaving when they hate or punish the self. Those that have killed need to have compassion for the abuse THEY suffered as children and in concurrent lifetimes. Their self-love or even acceptance of what they experienced will make them and consequently Gaia go lighter. Murderers dead and alive that want to move to greater light need to have compassion for the self.

Both groups of killers have NO COMPASSION for the brutality they suffered as children. There was NO SUPPORTIVE WITNESS that comforted them and told them how good they were and reassured them of their value. No one was there to demonstrate compassion, caring and acceptance for the brutalized infant and child. Because no one did that for you there is only one way now for you to go to greater lighter and understanding. You need to give your "child self" the compassion, caring and understanding you have always needed and wanted.

The Illuminati, religions, families and media tell us that we must "earn love" externally, compassion needs to come from outside of us and that is the LIE. Love, acceptance and compassion come from within us. We came to this planet to experience and learn to accept ourselves while living in a very dark, evil vibration. Movement to greater light and awareness is what will free you. Hating yourself and punishing the self only helps you go darker and darker. Nothing is gained that way and you put your own light out, your life force is drained. Have GREAT sympathy and compassion for the abused child you were in desperate need of compassion. As an adult you can be compassionate with you and heal the child. Give the child safety and the protection you did not have.

MORALITY and BELIEFS

Our morality, ethics and integrity are not based on "the facts" they are based on our VERY personal emotional experiences and what we have TOLD OURSELF about our experiences. The word or phrase you said to yourself during pivotal experiences is what you base your future beliefs and actions on. That includes the ones that make no sense. We may collect facts that can change our point of perception but we act on what we have told ourselves about any facts we gathered.

When things are too horrid or fearful to own and process we deny or make up a pleasant story more to our liking. This process starts in childhood when we feel our experiences a hundred times stronger than an adult would in the same situation.

80% or more children are abused physically, sexually and emotionally on earth. When you fail to remember your traumas you fail to have compassion for you and what you suffered. No compassion for you means NO COMPASSION for anyone else.

Dark leads the light into INTERNAL conflict. Who can I trust? Who will play nice? How can I protect myself? The internal conflict leads to fear and insecurity and fighting back. Internal conflict can also lead to creative solutions for dealing with trickery and deceit or trying to love the dark ones into lighter thoughts. The light child endlessly tries to win the darker parent over. With the unfairness of the dark, the light is provoked into creative solutions that are its own form of light. Lessons and experiences with dark gradually expand light's wisdom about how dark operates and what can and can't be done with dark.

LIES are frightened dark energy in the LIAR trying to deny what is truth. Lies, avoiding and deceiving chips away at an individual's self-worth by reducing the amount of compassion and respect they have for the self. Lies devalue the liar and fail to protect the liar or anyone else for that matter. Lies can create an illusion or prison without bars that enslaves the one not knowing the truth like most of us on earth or children in dysfunctional and abusive families. Being forced to interact with dark increases the compassion and understanding the light has for the fear, grandiosity and pretense that lives in dark people and cultures. They need to distort the truth to justify their irrational mean spirited thoughts and actions.

The dark ones have never had compassion for the wounds they suffered as innocent infants and children in this and their concurrent lives. So they lash out in their pain and anger hurting innocent ones the way they got wounded. Living in an old wound or fantasy or distraction is denial of the wounding you experienced. That wound locks you into repeating that pain and suffering over and over again without resolution. Having compassion for YOU the innocent that got tricked used, setup and abused is the only way to heal. Darkness teaches if you do not have compassion for you FIRST you will stay dark by doing what was done to you, wounding innocent ones and having the compulsion to repeat.

The endless worlds of the legion of light are "light on light" so there is little contrast or dark trickery, deceit and low self-esteem to observe or interact with. The reality of matter, the time lag of manifestation and the presence of dark are filled with the potential to gather wisdom not found in the endless world of light on light without deceit and mistrust. The place we all came from. ALL CREATION is made up of light with wide varieties of frequencies of light that range from no light to a 100% light. Our physical body is over 90% space and the rest is resonating light patterned by our thought forms. The collective group we live within and our individual thoughts create the mental and emotional construct of our reality down to the smallest detail and quanta. Our emotional beliefs are handed down from our ancestors and altered by our childhood and adult life experiences.

There is a special relationship between the biology and the soul aspect. They REFLECT each other and exist within each other. This layering and reflecting is the result of the invisible wanting to see and understand itself by slowing things down and becoming matter. The LEGION of LIGHT wanted to learn more about its creation and it self. To increase the legion of lights awareness about its creation they used contrast or duality to bring out the extreme coping behaviors of those on the opposing side. In duality and linear time the cause, (your thought) and the affect, what your thought created becomes clear. The physical world is considered the legion of lights laboratory that slows down the ability of humans and soul aspects to manifest what they think and the results of that thought.

Some light ones were assigned the role of being dark for a period of time to experience contrast or opposition. The dark creator called itself Anchara and those choosing more dark than light worked with and for Anchara. On the side of light was Michael for those starting out with more light than dark. Over the millions of years all participating entities have experienced all the various degrees of lightness and dark at one time or another so it didn't matter what you started up with you experienced both sides as much as you wanted to.

Hopefully the wisdom you gained has put you back into more light than dark as this cycle of learning has been completed.

In the beginning the dark were told to rule the Milky Way Galaxy by force, deceit and tyranny. Many dark empires were formed and slave races were created to do their bidding. The light was peaceful, productive with high vibrational societies living in harmony and equality. Could they maintain the higher vibration with the dark tormenting them? Would the dark encourage the light to join them? The forces of Anchara felt they needed to destroy and take what they wanted and the galactic wars were under way. Wars ravaged our galaxy for 20 million years. Just as there is always some war going on all the time ravaging the earth. Just as there are unending disputes with family members and clans. That is the way of it with dark or limited consciousness they are fearful, easily lied to and want to be told what to do. They are always looking for a higher authority and personal power.

Our galaxy has large cracks in the fabric of space and time from all the energy wars. Light and dark engaged in endless high tech battles. Endless conflicts allowed the dark ones to move on the light ones using trickery and deceit. The way many parents interact with their children and prepare them to use trickery and deceit in their life. The manipulator and manipulated acted as mirrors for each other. The parent, country or Anchara group pretended to have the same goals and objectives as the light did to get the child, country or light group to trust the dark and think it was their friend. They suck you in with a lie and then switch to their hidden agenda.

The game of contrast officially ended with the Treaty of Anchara in 1995 when the Alliance of Anchara finally agreed to relinquish its claims to earth and they agreed to move to grater light. The few remaining dark fleets retreated to their home-worlds on the far side of the Milky Way Galaxy. There are individuals and small groups refusing to move to more light so the light side has changed the rules of engagement in the energy war of dark and light on earth. As of May 21, 2011 the angelic realm is taking measures to release and prevent dark on earth. Rainbow and Crystal souls only incarnate into biologies or parents with more light than dark.

Children born to those with less than 36% light will not have a soul. The infant will have flat affect and act like "no one is home" or empty and it will feel like having a doll or robot to interact with. This means the caretaker will not be able to torment, steal or harness their FEAR energy. Soulless children are not expected to survive past 2020 because of the higher vibrations on Gaia at that time. These children will not make it much past infancy and will be born with diseases and other health issues. As dark souls are dying off or leaving the planet they are not being replaced with other dark souls. To incarnate on earth now you need to carry more light than dark.

Souls with more dark than light are not allowed to incarnate on earth any longer. That means that dark ancestors can no longer incarnate into biology. No new dark ones can enter and that means many frustrated very dark souls waiting to incarnate from the 4th dimension are making the spiritual atmosphere around earth dense with their anxiety, anger and tension. Mediums and ghost whisperers will be very helpful if they are willing to explain to these souls how things have changed and help them to accept that they will not be incarnating on earth. Help the confused souls to the bridge of flowers or a portal of greater light so they can be cared for and relocated.

One third of the children on earth are being raised in the trauma based programming of the illuminati or Satanists. The Illuminati needs something with a soul for their rituals to harness the energy and allow demonic entities to possess slaves to open different dimensions. The Illuminati has a great many "breeders" or females they imprison and forced to have babies that never get into "the system" so the public is not aware of their existence. Frequently these are VERY young girls. The breeders will probably be killed in a ritual the way most are when the illuminati is done with you. The illuminati will need to step up their kidnapping operations or buying infants with souls to keep functioning as usual.

The illuminati use's the PERSONALITY ASSESSMENT SYSTEM / PAS that was designed by John Gittinger to evaluate the infant's current and future personality and abilities. There are 3 major axes that can be graphed to describe a child's personality. Then programming is done in that direction with 6-month goals to develop the new mind-controlled slave. For example, the programmers would know the child would become a social or religious reformer. The child's programming charts would then be labeled some suitable occupation such as "Environmental Activist", "Pentecostal church reformer", "Consumer Advocate", or "Activist against Narcotics" so they can push the illuminati's agenda.

Light is working hard to shut down access from the dark ones to those who are committed to going lighter. Communication from dark ones is being blocked and can break down phones and computers.

Chapter 3
OUR LEADERS CHILDHOODS

Close to a third of infants on earth throughout their childhood have experienced "trauma based programming" that is designed so you will NOT consciously remember what happened to you. Trauma happens many times daily to these children. The ADULT CHILD of trauma-based programming functions in a dissociated state most of the time. They have been trained NOT to think for themselves. Most of the people in powerful positions in the world were raised with "trauma based programming" and are adult children of this programming the same as their parents are. They are the Illuminati or the top of the pyramid of Freemasons or Mormons or KKK or Jesuit Priests the list is endless. They lack awareness of and compassion for their endless childhood traumas, control and abuses. That makes it easy for them to be controlled, do as they are told to do and robotically inflict pain and suffering on the innocent.

Freemasonry hides information from its members on the bottom of the pyramid because if they knew the truth most would run the other direction. The top of the pyramid is hard-core Satanists and illuminati. To communicate and share their body of secrets, the Illuminati leaders and members use symbols. The leaders have different meanings for the rites, ceremonies and hand signs than those on the lower levels of the pyramid. The abusive parent, family, clan or cult also has secrets, ceremonies and signs for the child they are betraying, and abusing one more time.

Throughout human history, marks, signs, pictures, and hieroglyphs were used to convey words, ideas, concepts, and secrets. The elite use many symbols and signs to hide their magic and unethical behaviors and beliefs. For example in the very first-degree ritual to become a Freemason the Entered Apprentice is blindfolded and a cable-tow is hung around his neck to symbolically say they are dumb or the candidate is hoodwinked. His or her superiors have intentionally set out to deceive the candidate through all the ritual degrees up to and including the 33rd degree Freemason. What is most important to know in Masonry or the illuminati is not taught openly. The true wisdom is concealed and hidden until each Mason seeks revelation and discerns the TRUTH for the SELF. There are no interpretations of the Rituals for the participants about the deceptive practices used.

The Mason or illuminati symbols are displayed and flaunted in our media for all to see. The leaders are making fun of our ignorance or hoodwinking us when they display their signs and messages in plain sight. Most people are dissociated or in a trance and do not SEE or they "buy into the lie" about what is really being conveyed and how they work against our freedom. Their secrets are concealed in plain sight tricking the innocent. Always, we must discern the TRUTH for the SELF. Make the many little moves in thought needed to get things rolling to increase your awareness and prove your commitment to understanding more. God, the legion of light or your mom cannot do it for you. It must be your own creation.

The Council on Foreign Relations whose 3,000 members run almost every facet of our federal government, especially at the top is "trauma based programmed adult children." The United Nations endorsed and funded by our Congress is headed up the inner circle of the Illuminati. Other illuminati run organizations are Rand Corporation, Hughes Aircraft, Northrop Corporation, General Electric, AT & T, Sandia Corporation, Stanford Research Institute, Colorado School of Mines, Walsh Construction, Bechtel Corporation winning massive contracts to rebuild Iraq.

There are 13 ruling Illuminati FAMILIES on earth and each family is given an area of the earth and a function to perform. Their functions are global finance, development of military technology, mind control, media and religion. Each ruling family has a council of 13. All 13 families are hybrids 50% human DNA and 50% or more reptilian DNA. The layer below the 13 ruling families in the hierarchy, support the ruling families and are called the Committee of 300.

These families are the generational illuminati satanic bloodlines and the power behind the secret societies, most governments, the sciences and religions on earth. They direct their operations from behind the scenes on and in earth, the moon and Mars. The adult child of trauma-based programming follows orders and gets "rewards" for good behavior. The reward is generally financial and sexual and often twisted. People are so well trained, fearful and robotic in the Illuminati that they can do their tasks WITHOUT THOUGHT or MEMORY of doing what they do. Illuminati programming is designed to make the child and adult feel worthless UNLESS they are serving their masters when and how they want to be served.

When you forget what shaped your belief systems it is not so easy to adjust those beliefs because you are not aware you have them or why. Conscious awareness of what shaped your beliefs might horrify you and make it easy for you to see the self-destructive beliefs you were forced to adopt as a survival mechanism because of the cruel insensitive environment you were raised in as a child. The illuminati train all their children to please without any thought for themselves. They do not want their children to think for themselves or know what they feel. They do not want them to bond with anyone or anything other than their handlers the "cult family" or illuminati.

When any group or individual encourages you to suspend your thought and feeling be alert for the lies and deceptions that will surely follow. Dark individuals, businesses and groups all operate the same way with the same modus operandi. They give you the lie that they will solve any issue you have. They take your money and your trust to seduce you into allowing them to "take control" of your thought and body. After that they suck the life out of you and say, "You wanted it." You asked for help and you got it. The group or individual frequently a parent run their form of sexual addiction or abuse on the infant, child or adult putting the individual in overwhelm FIRST. That is the dark pattern established in childhood and carried on throughout life by the wide variety of predators available on earth.

When an infant, child or adult is overwhelmed they dissociate giving up their control to their predator or actor (legal term found in America's penal codes). The only way to end the cycle of dark taking advantage of you is to stay conscious and aware of what is happening and how it feels to you. Always evaluate what you hear and experience, does it sound and feel right? THINK for your self. Until you are willing to "be conscious" and stop dissociating you will be in the company of other dark unconscious individuals that are more than willing to run your life, siphon your energy and use your body. On this planet of free will there is NO ONE here to rescue you other than you. When someone dose offer to be responsible for you it is a lie.

ACTING OUT and ADDICTION

The large majority of the population is unconscious and sexually acting out. Sexual addiction is the largest addiction in the world. Sexual acting out and obsessive sexual activity even done alone like obsessive masturbation or use of pornography is sexual addiction. Abuse and sexual addiction is present in all dark groups and individuals. Drugs and "possession" by a dark entity are used to encourage you to do things that are against your conscious beliefs. When you lose control, dissociate and abandon your biology, feelings and thought you will be used.

America has laws on the books or the "penal code" of what is and isn't legal. The penal code or criminal code defines sexual misconduct as when he or she engages in sexual intercourse or oral sexual conduct or anal sexual conduct or engages in sexual conduct with an animal or a dead human body or with another person without such person's consent. A person is guilty of rape in the first degree when he or she engages in sexual intercourse with another person by force or they are incapable of consent by reason of being physically helpless; or they are less than eleven years old.

A person is guilty of forcible touching when such person intentionally, and for no legitimate purpose, forcibly touches the sexual or other intimate parts of another person: for the purpose of degrading or abusing such person; or gratifying the actor's sexual desire. Forcible touching includes the squeezing, grabbing or pinching of such other person's sexual or other intimate parts.

A person is guilty of aggravated sexual abuse in the fourth degree when: He or she inserts a foreign object in the vagina, urethra, penis or rectum of another person and the other person is incapable of consent by reason of being less than seventeen years old.

A person is guilty of female genital mutilation when: a person knowingly circumcises, excises, or infibulates the whole or any part of the labia majora or labia minora or clitoris of another person who has not reached eighteen years of age; or being a parent, guardian or other person legally responsible and charged with the care or custody of a child less than eighteen years old.

A person is guilty of facilitating a sex offense with a controlled substance when he or she: knowingly and unlawfully possesses a controlled substance and administers such substance to another person without such person's consent and with intent to commit against such person conduct constituting a felony defined in this article for the purpose, in whole or substantial part, of his or her own direct sexual gratification.

All children raised with trauma-based programming have suffered all of the above and much worse from birth on. Illuminati members raised this way are in the top positions of control throughout the world and are not punished for their almost daily abuses of force and control. They hold top positions in the military and police force, religions and in the court and medical systems. There is documentation in the book Brice Taylor wrote THANKS for the MEMORIES, she was used as a presidential sex toy and personal computer.

Breeders are chosen from childhood to breed children according to bloodlines or given in arranged marriages or cult alliances to ELEVATE the child's DNA to be more reptilian or have babies for sacrifice there is NO birth certificate or record of the birth. Some breeders live underground as prisoners. All the children starting at two years old are trained as prostitutes or sex slaves to any adult presented to them. Child pornography, snuff films and illegal drugs are big business and large moneymakers for the illuminati throughout the world. Child couriers all around the world run guns, money, drugs, or illegal artifacts across state or national boundaries. Behavioral scientists oversee the illuminati training in local and regional groups and are intensely involved in data collection and human experimentation just as our government is and always has been during the 1900s and it hasn't stopped.

Abuse creates cold insensitive, DISSOCIATED people that don't empathize or think much about cause and affect when they do not have compassion for the pain they suffered. When your awareness is of being confused because your reality is splintered and you are force feed lies, drugged, electric shocked regularly to keep your programs aligned with their agenda your existence is about surviving one more assault. The confused state and being fearful of more pain physically and emotionally enable you to react without question or thought. All the adult children have handlers to control them. The handlers are internal and external and the adult child is frequently not aware they are being handled.

Around the world the political leaders, the most popular media and news people that are very bright and verbal are sent to journalism school and will work for local or regional media upon graduation to write books and articles sympathetic to the Illuminati viewpoint without ever know themselves to be raised with trauma-based programming. Most all the famous entertainers are children raised in the illuminati trauma based programming. You cannot get to the top of anything in a world run by darkness unless you are a compliant worker for their agenda consciously or unconsciously.

Judith Spencer wrote the true WELL DOCUMENTED story of how easy it was for a town in America to be taken over and run by Satanists in her book "Satan's High Priest." How catering to and supporting the sexual perversion and abuse in the town's members along with all their other addictions created a solid financial base to control the town and its citizens. Trauma based programming for children born to Satanists and then the sexual abuse that goes on in a dysfunctional family you have most children in the town being abused physically and sexually. Many parents of these children are not consciously aware of their children's programming or their own programming. The more important a person is to the illuminati agenda the greater number of controllers they have internally and externally. The public sees them as heroes, lucky and important movers and shakers. They are as controlled and manipulated as any human robot can be.

Dark people, the large majority of people on earth consider a child a piece of property they can do whatever they want to do to it. Abuse of children is what gives us our criminals and dysfunctional adults. How can an abused child know what is right and function in a healthy way? They grow up wounded, angry and act out. When they get access to a child they frequently do what was done to them. The average cult member or illuminati adult and our criminals function emotionally and socially at the 3 to 4 year old level. So how do they demonstrate adult compassionate nurturing behavior to their children? They don't. Certainly they do not know how to nurture the self either and so goes the cycle. Sexual acting out is used to distract you from your anxiety, fear and overwhelming emotions.

All the experts agree severe child abuse is the childhood of all monsters and criminals. All children raised with trauma do not become monsters but all monsters were raised with traumas. To move out of that control or programming a person needs to want to take control of them self and their thoughts. Your many little choices to allow your handlers to control you hold you in the reality you are in. Change your reality by owning it.

Our individual world is our creation that changes or stays the same as a result of our thoughts and beliefs and ability to STAY CONSCIOUS and aware of what we are doing. When you stay aware of what you do "all the time" and monitor your thoughts you can break your programming cycle. THINK and decide for yourself what you want to do. Break the dark hold on you by feeling, thinking and staying in present time. The thoughts you hold close and nurture are the ones you are creating your reality with. It matters not if the thought started with you or another. You are in control of your own brain and mind that you feed thoughts to and hold. Decide what thoughts you want to stay focused on. Fear, worry and upset feed the dark. Become aware of your feelings and notice your thoughts. Wondering about our imperfections and thoughts take us on an interesting journey of curiosity that maintains our enthusiasm for this experience. New beliefs show up to challenge old beliefs and increase our enthusiasm. Stagnating in old patterns, thoughts and relationships diminish enthusiasm for life.

JEALOUSY is ATTACHMENT

ENVY and JEALOUSY are about you thinking someone or something else is getting what YOU believe you should be getting from another or a source outside yourself. So you start whining, pouting, plotting and complaining in an effort to guilt or force the other to give it to you. Our prisons are full of people thinking others OWE them. When you do manage to get what you THINK you need from another it is NEVER enough or long lasting enough to make you feel what you are missing out on. You have also given your power and energy to another person, entity or event to fill your little human needs and wants. Your attachment to wanting or taking something from another takes their freedom away and MISDIRECTS your thoughts. There is NOTHING you can acquire externally that will make your insides feel better.

The belief you hold and attachment to anyone or anything in the 3rd or 4th dimension is misdirected. The only one that can give you what you need all the time the way you want it is your connection with your soul aspects. A child, parent, friend or anything forced from anyone can't give you what you continuously long for. Many enjoy creating all kinds of drama about how they have been wronged, abused, ripped off and "no one loves me." Just like the child that throws a drama to get sugar that will throw its body out of balance and escalate their inability to manage their actions. They demand, pout and whine to get what fails to please their soul. They please a biological imbalance when it's the spiritual misalignment that needs rebalance. The soul craves the peace and calm that alignment with universal law gives the little human.

You need to stay in your biology and prioritize your thoughts. We ALL have the skill set to do that. What imbalances you have attracted you have to UNDO yourself. When you force a child (or anyone) to please you in any way you go against universal law "give and receive only compassion" and you worship (give your power away to) another by controlling them to please your darker vibrational truths. That is also against "The universal law of ALLOWING." You are attached to and forcing an outcome. Allowing requires granting all, even your child the right to BE just as they are. They do not need the dark truths of your force and control reinforced.

Even the Holy Bible commands: "Thou shalt have no other gods before ME," (not even refined sugar) (Exodus 20:3) and "Thou shall not covet thy neighbor's house, wife, manservant, maidservant, ox, or ass. (Exodus 20:17) You shouldn't ask others to fill your needs or wants because you need to do it for yourself. That is your job alone. Following others or seducing or forcing things from others is worship of the person or thing like the "golden idols" the Jews worship. The Ten Commandments are the universal laws simplified as "rules" to point out what is a dark and light choice. Those that believe self-love happens externally and not internally will always covet and not allow others their freedom.

Universal laws are generated from the legion of light's ONLY commandment "Give and receive only unconditional love and compassion." That is how we can keep our individual world balanced and harmonious. This law governs all situations and especially your morality. Working within the laws assures a positive outcome eventually even while living on a dark planet. Going against the laws creates suffering not always immediately to strongly point out there are other options of greater balance and harmony for you to consider.

Children are literally mature souls in a smaller biology. The parent never owns the child, their biology or soul. They have accepted responsibility to care for the child and grant them their freedom. A child is not your life long personal friend to jerk around forever even if that is what your parent did to you. That is why it is wise to avoid reproduction until you have your life in order, so you have something other than more abuse to give your child.

The unconscious dark ones haunt themselves with their cycles of negative behavior that never change, never bring joy or new thoughts. The cycles or repetitious behavior patterns were created to avoid feeling your pain. The dark ones nurture their old wounds not remembering how and when they received them. They drag the betrayal and trauma of the past to haunt them in present time. They are locked in a time capsule of their own unconscious suffering to avoid feeling their original pain. The journey from fear, suffering and old wounds to compassion for the self is the journey that needs taking to leave duality. Your soul aspects can read in your aura the information you need to know and feel, just ask them.

Illusion is only found in the 3rd and lower 4th dimensional realities. Since fear is key to holding you in this dark illusion know that fear leaves you when you gather more knowledge and compassion for you first. Expanding to the upper 4th and 5th dimension makes it EASIER for you to discern what is illusional and what is truth. A common tool used to heal present time suffering and raising your vibration is to heal your past wounds or suffering. Free yourself of old mental programs handed down to you from family and country by questioning what you do. Release emotional pain stored in your biology and your aura or your personal Akashic Records by owning the truth of what you have experience. Acceptance of what has happened to you, your feelings about it and embracing it increases your spiritual wisdom and vibration.

Some subtle cues that you are moving to higher vibrations are that you tire easily of endless drama, intrigue and deception. Violence, competition, gossip and adrenaline filled experiences loose their glamour and entertainment value. Secrets are counterproductive and benefit no one except those with dark agendas. You are finally able to allow others to do it "their way" to do what is best for them. Knowledge makes us aware of the futility of opposition, war and forcing others in the family, community and the country. Some foods become too heavy to digest and wearing synthetic materials will become more uncomfortable. Our biology is struggling to adapt to the ever-rising frequencies of earth and our increasing awareness of universal truths.

The higher frequency that heals our biology also creates exhaustion in our body as the new brain connections and carbon based chemistry transforms into a crystalline-based biology. Our awareness is resonating to a much higher frequency than the biology is accustomed to and that is tiring. Frequent naps and spending time in nature helps rebalance you. The frequency of earth is now higher than it has been since the fall of Atlantis and the transmutation of physical matter into spiritual energies are happening slow and steadily. Unity of your awareness is expansion of your consciousness seeing all the connections we have to others and the different elements of Gaia's body we connect with.

When others irritate or upset you look inside you to locate that part of you that you disapprove of. Find the fear or darkness you carry that has magnetized your attention to their "FAULT" in your judgment of them. They are reflecting a fear or judgment you have made about yourself. When you can own that part of you and have compassion for that aspect of you, the judgment will stop.

In the sixth dimension all reality is awareness. Having a form is like changing clothes for us. Releasing the need to have a form means liberation from the illusions of space, time and opposites. You can simultaneously be aware of and live in multiple realities in other dimensions and galaxies its like the multi-tasking we do now.

Many children's "imaginary friends" are really their soul aspects perceived through their imagination or 5th dimensional thought. Imagination is the mental activity that connects us to our innate awareness and the only socially acceptable way to go in the 3rd dimension. Higher vibrational truths are us "being creative" as that is more fun and enjoyable than watching someone else entertain you.

Chapter 4
ENABLING is OVER NOW

SERVICE to OTHERS, caretaking and enabling is over now. Compassion for YOU needs to be first. Then the compassion you give others is pure and supportive. When you don't care for you first what you give is tainted with your neediness, dark, negativity or unconsciousness. Our beliefs dictate our behavior and feelings. As long as you believe you are here on earth to SERVE the need of any other you will create more of what you have already experienced. Caretaking and service to others first has been glamorized especially by religions to keep us in line and working hard for the top of the pyramid or our needy parent, spouse or boss. Caretaking, enabling and service to others first is a way to blackmail others into valuing you because you have been taught NOT to value yourself. When you sacrifice for another that is very tainted and poisonous to the one you gift your sacrifice too.

Commonly we surrender individual thought and responsibility when we join a group. Wisdom and allowing can only be learned and mastered individually. "Group think" and sacrifice are tools used by the dark to control and force. The more you serve, care take or force the less freedom the other has to be what they want to be and the less freedom YOU have to be what you want to be. Allowing is unconditional love for you first and allowing others to do as they wish first. Allowing is the knowledge that everything is as it ought to be.

We attract what we focus on and allow that to come into our reality. When you have doubt, fear, or worry and that vibration dominates that is what you create and allow by default. For example you fear you will be abandoned again and your low vibration and focus attracts that to you yet again. You have not yet realized that your soul never abandons you and your answers and comfort are within.

Darkness does not believe in allowing anyone free choice, they think that is dangerous to their agenda. Even the dark leaders are controlled and forced by the dark dictators above them. "Your dark mom" is controlled by "her dark mom" that is why as a world we have been "the worker bees" and operate under the motto we have been given of "service to others first." That belief of service to others first prevents you from having compassion for YOU first. Compassion for the self starts happening when you carry more than 60% light. Honoring the self-FIRST and your biology is being in alignment with universal law. Unconditional love and compassion is the highest frequency there is and it needs to start with you loving yourself first. The unawakened think they are victims or predators or servants and their purpose is to suffer, kill, control or be victimized. Awakening spiritually is YOU knowing you are a soul pretending to be human temporarily. Being one that allows frees you of your negativity, unconsciousness and patterns of low vibration.

The universal law of DIVINE MANIFESTATION is win-win-win-win to benefit all involved and harm to none. Any harm to another in the process or outcome of creation is not DIVINE and carries karmic debt. When you are not allowing you are resisting or pushing against and that is the dark unconscious negative behavior that has become a "normal natural pattern of darkness" on earth. When your immediate emotional reaction is to control, blame or force someone else's behavior, stop and remind yourself they don't need your evaluation of them or a course correction from you! There is freedom in allowing and not enabling others to be who they are and allowing circumstances to be what they are.

A pretty story to replace painful reality has never healed anyone. Many people seek help because they are suffering. When they want to heal something they give a pretty story instead of the truth. The wounded person and the helper try to heal the "pretty story" and they are surprised that nothing gets healed or rebalanced. Some of the most popular pretty stories are, I had a happy childhood. My parent(s) love me. She or he beats me everyday but they love me. We are a close family. My parent was over protective not needy and controlling. Denial of your personal reality prevents you from healing. There is no need to heal a story a child made up to deal with overwhelming negative energy. The stumbling block in all therapy is trying to heal a pretty story instead of the individual's real experience.

You can only heal what is or was true for that person. Pretty stories get started in childhood. The fairytales we read children reinforce pretty stories and support "Magic thinking." Stories and movies have a child or adult saving all of humanity or their clan or their family or town with one heroic act and they all live happily ever after. That story line has never been true and never will be true. One person cannot "do it" for others. We each need to do it for our self.

Remember this planet has a very dark bias and the vast majority of parents are more dark than light. Self hate and pathology starts at home and is nurtured at home. A child feels their experiences a hundred times more intensely than an adult having the same experience. Children telepathically read and SENSE the negative energy people in the family are projecting and that can easily put the infant or child in overwhelm. When something overwhelms the child they dissociate, detach or disengage from the reality they are in. Denial of too many painful experiences leads one to not experiencing their reality consciously because they move to a dissociated state most of the time they are awake. When a memory or emotion does come to their awareness they unconsciously turn it into a physical pain or symptom. Their senses shut down along with the mental ability to process what is happening. But the feelings get stored in the body and physical symptoms develop. Without conscious memory a pretty story is created.

AN EXAMPLE The parent never wanted the child and mentally and emotionally blames the child for existing. The child is an emotional burden to the parent that never resolved their issues of being a burden emotionally to their parents, before they became a parent them self. The new parent will be passing on the family pathology to their child when they reproduce the same style of parenting they got. Words may or may not be expressed but the infant and child telepathically gets the message. They get the message when they are treated roughly or ignored or your tone is harsh. Each time the parent and child interact the child is painfully aware of the parent's blame, upset and anger. For the infant to stay alive with that much negative energy they dissociate. They are powerless to defend them self in any other way. As the child ages it might be depressed, angry or act out. The child creates pretty stories because they do not consciously remember or it is too painful to own the truth.

The self-talk would go something like this, if I don't cry, or I am a good helper or I get good grades my parent will feel kindly towards me. By adulthood the "adult child" will say to others, I was a happy good child and my parents loved me. My question to the "adult child" is why are you suffering physically and confused mentally?

ANOTHER EXAMPLE the parent is lonely, isolated, self-absorbed and has no friends. The infant came into their life to fix and heal all the parents suffering. The child telepathically senses the consuming neediness of the parent and knows it is their job to rescue and fix that parent. Oh that is not overwhelming for a child! Adults run away from that type of person. The infant or child dissociates from the burden they carry. They are physically, emotionally and frequently mentally trapped. The child is not allowed to spend time with others because the parent wants a companion to watch TV with or shop with or golf with. The adult shares all their adult problems and issues inappropriately with the small child. The adult money fears are shared and scare the child. The emotional I hate "so and so" anger and wounding gets shared. What child should be forced to deal with all that hate? The child hears that no one loves or treats the adult right and that increases the child's burden and desire to kill or rescue the parent.

The adult child tells pretty stories like, Mother and I are very close. Dad and I do everything together. My parent was over protective of me or controlled me. And the adult child is lonely, isolated, self absorbed and has no friends. They do have their needy parent, spouse or child to keep happy.

ANOTHER EXAMPLE the parent or older sibling "in charge" is angry and cruel. Sensing that overwhelmed the child and they dissociated most of the time. The denial of reality and the resulting pretty story may go like this. My parents were busy earning money for me because they loved me. They allowed me the freedom to do what ever I wanted to do. My parents weren't around much but they loved me and I had a good childhood. SO, why are you suffering physically and confused mentally?

RITUAL and PRAYER

Mantras, prayers and rituals sometimes hypnotize and always ENTRAIN the members of the ritual or mantra and or prayer. Entrainment for those with low levels of light or vibration means they dissociate and generally stop thinking for them self to play "follow the leader or bully" along with having their light or energy siphoned. Those that carry low levels of light tend to focus on their "feelings of lack" and they pray and bargain to get things or stuff they can get and do for the self. The illuminati operation has rituals for everything and everyone that also include all manner of drugs, electric shock and manipulation.

We have had many dark lifetimes of codependency or being the victim and predator. To change or evolve out of those patterns of dark the human needs to take the lead and break their dark contracts with other souls by telling their dark soul aspects NO MORE. When you follow a dark leader or family member things can really get dark and dysfunctional.

Old spiritual masters could be entrained with and have as many as 1,000 feeding cords to different followers. Moses was entrained with the Jews from Egypt but towards the end of his life his truths became darker as he pulled away from universal law. Moses was never able to convey the power and importance of self-love that comes from within us to the Israelites. Moses used his energy to manifest miracles like the parting of the Red Sea that amazed and entertained his followers. The followers believed you needed to earn self-worth externally. Like parents that give children presents instead of fulfilling their emotional needs.

Those individuals carrying mid ranges of light (40 to 60%) find mantras, prayers and rituals comforting and they offer the illusion of unity or the feeling of being SPECIAL. Some rituals are just fun like Christmas and Hanukah.

Those that carry a lot of light and have a high vibration find that mantras, prayers and rituals get in the way and are not appropriate or in alignment with the universal law.

Self-love happens internally never externally. Those that believe self-love happens externally and not internally will always "covet" or yearn to possess, not allowing others their freedom. Those that worship external "authority" give away their energy, power, thinking and frequently their biology and health.

External results of an action are not significant. The inner character change during a challenging struggle is what matters. Going against the laws creates suffering to strongly point out there are other options of greater balance and harmony for you to consider. The legion of light is the Intelligence behind all creation that exists only in present time. We experience different realities in different dimensions to increase our own spiritual understanding of what is light. The physical world and our struggles with matter, biology and dark truths are temporary challenges or educational tools and learning experiences.

The higher vibrating soul groups that have incarnated for the past 35 years have made a large shift with their increased light and spiritual beliefs that have held their parents, schools, religions and institutions to a higher standard. The children being born in the Middle East and America are not able to accept the hate and vengeance their parents handed down to them. There is a new type of socialization and communication among those under the age of 35 because they trust each other more than they do the older generation that worships money, things, stuff, punishment and control. The older generation plays "follow the leader," pray a lot, reinforce many rituals and are patriotic and nationalistic. The stuck energy of dictators, dark leaders or bullies or abusers or tyrants uses hierarchies of dissociated ones under them to control and force.

With the revolution of consciousness going on their structures are starting to crumble or malfunction. Their oppressive darkness is getting unstuck and transmuted because the dissociated are waking up and having compassion for them self. New answers are being created and implemented. They use telepathy and are more in alignment with universal law then their older relatives. They are socially conscious.

When you ask a Syrian, Libyan or Egyptian or anyone what they want, they want choice and abundance in one form or another. The broader definition of abundance is NOURISHMENT for each day, one day at a time in the now moment. War attracts more war, fighting attracts more fighting and leads to sorrow, death, destruction and suffering. Awareness of how those dark truths FEEL makes us choose to be friendly and accepting. During the transition and transmutation from conflict to peaceful coexistence there is always some turbulent energy.

Transmutation is the process of raising the frequency of a person, place, thing or situation. Spiritual transmutation is the act of raising your frequency or vibration step by step to that of light and compassion. You change your thoughts and inner reality so that what appears to be dark moves back into its original frequency of light. The transmutation process starts within you by you identifying your lower frequency thoughts, emotions and reactions. We consciously pick the thoughts we hold and our emotional reactions to those thoughts. Important information comes from fearful thoughts and emotion. But putting your focus on martyrdom or victimization you are staying in a low vibration. You must personally experience or have in your awareness that particular truth or darkness prior to transmuting it to align with "give and receive only compassion."

Dark and light are a matter of perception or "what your focus" is. Discern what person, place, thing or situation is dark and walk away. Then perceive the light in what you focus on. Through selective perception and alignment with the laws of attraction and allowing the light expands beyond the darkness. This is NOT denial because nothing goes away or is transmuted when it is denied. Owning and accepting makes dark dissipate not denial.

FEAR VICTIMIZES the SELF

Fear is the lowest frequency or vibration and only found in the 3rd and lower 4th dimension. Fear is ALMOST as powerful a creational force as compassion even though it is not real in higher vibrations. In fear we automatically VICTIMIZE the SELF and attract more fear to us. The little human thinks fear is real and it is to the biology. Loss of the biology rather than surrendering to darkness is fine with your soul. Neutralize your fear and heal it with more information and COMPASSION for you first. Fear is the unknown or lack of information and never the opposite of love. As we walk through our fears and worries we transmute fear into something more useful. Fear withholds love for the self.

We are transitioning into a different frequency emotionally, physically and spiritually BUT things and some people around us continue to appear as they were. We think and feel differently but mostly look the same because the transition is internal and moving incrementally. It is all about what you think. The process of transition is clearing out old stuck beliefs by owning them and seeing the higher vibrational truth or bigger picture. Our soul aspect presents "in code" or with "clues" or in dreams our wounds and unconscious UNRESOLVED issues to own release or "clear out" by seeing the larger picture. What you have avoided thinking about or been unaware of needs to be brought into your conscious awareness. Unresolved issues we have carried in our aura for all our lifetimes need to see the light. Our "unconscious mind" or lack of awareness will no longer be used or needed in higher vibrations. We will be aware of everything all the time and choose what to give special attention.

The unconscious place, thing, people or events hidden from your awareness create fear in you. Increased knowledge about them releases your fear and that increases your spiritual wisdom and frequency. Darkness is light that has taken on too much fear, pain and suffering. ALL your pockets of density need to lighten up and dissipate.

Defensive posture or living in a low-grade state of fear creates disintegration and drains our spiritual energy and physical strength. Energy does not follow form your thought and "energy focus" create the form in the shape of a person, place, thing, emotion or situation. Eventually we will be able to see how the energy takes shape. When we see energy start coalescing into a form we will be able to alter it on the spot. The way you can stop a fight before it gets started when you read the signs that the energy is going in that direction. The thoughts and emotion we carry create our thought forms.

Earth has always been a reality filled with many creative expressions of Gaia's awareness. Many civilizations began, grew, ascended or fell. At great risk to Her planetary body she has been patient with the wants of her humans as they increased their spiritual wisdom by learning through cause and affect. Those who have used their creations for selfish control and manipulation have lowered the frequency of Gaia to the point of near-extinction. Once you fully understand and accept that your human form is as much a part of earth as a tree or a mountain your awareness and creator abilities expand. Our biology is a vehicle to share with 3rd and 4th dimensional elements of Gaia's body. What we create for our self is created for the planet also. Humans are portals that allow the frequencies of the universe to enter Gaia's core. What is done to others is done to the self and the planet.

Whatever Gaia creates for Her planet self, she creates for everyone and thing on and in the planet.

We perceived our self as an individual or an island on a planet and our expanded awareness makes us a planet that lives in a Galaxy. As we start to enter new frequencies we have other Galaxy members offering to show us around and fill gaps in our knowledge. There are many versions of reality and many versions of life on earth and in the galaxy. The different versions are actually different states of awareness. When our consciousness expands into higher frequencies we are no longer trapped by our fear, ignorance or limited though. Communication is expanded to pictures, tones, feelings and increasing physical sensations.

In the beginning the legion of light creates oversouls that create souls. Each soul starts out with 5 aspects or parts. A new aspect gets created and added to the 5 aspects as they go through challenging experiences in a reality or matrix or illusion to gather spiritual wisdom or have greater understanding of how to give and receive only compassion. A soul needs to gather higher truths and an additional 15 to 20 more aspects BEFORE they can incarnate into duality with biology on a "planet of free will" like earth. You need that much experience in compassion and wisdom gathering to experience what darkness or unconsciousness or negativity can teach you about you and your essence or morality or core personality. Or your dark thought and behavior patterns will eventually consume your life force.

Sometimes the soul aspect in biology or human, goes stagnant, gets stubborn or is too fearful to change their dark experiences. The childhood traumas have put them in a constant state of fear and dissociation and their belief is that change will kill them because they are only biology without a soul. Being dark is the only way to keep the biology alive. When that happens the soul group will try to still benefit from the experience with biology on earth. They will set up a transfer of soul aspects that all agree on. The stagnant soul will leave and a slightly higher vibrating soul aspect will move into the biology. The new soul aspect will have awareness of the firsts' souls history but not be emotionally invested in it the way the first soul was.

2 to 4 soul aspects follow the human into negative or unconscious thought and behavior to hold the connection to the human and the other soul aspects. This group of 2 to 4 soul aspects will be operating in the low vibrational band the human has chosen for it self and they will line up synchronicities in that band of vibration for the human to experience. The aspect transfer process can happen overnight, take months or years to complete when the original essence resists the change. When the biology gets overwhelmed and chooses to shut down, during a traumatic incident, during a coma or accident there can be an aspect transfer. There are billions of souls who need or want to

come here at this time. Some for a short period of time to create resolution from previous experiences or they may have a great deal of wisdom to offer the population on earth. What they have to offer needs to come from an articulate adult rather than a dependent child, walk-ins occur mostly in adult situations. It is rare for a walk-in to take place for a child but it happens.

Soul aspect transfers are happening to 80% of the population on earth now to help raise each human's vibration. The percentage is so high because so many are stuck in the illusion of duality, abuse and their biology is all they have. The dark behavior started a great many life times ago for the little human and is still rather dark. Our babies and children have not been honored or treated well throughout the ages so they grow up and repeat the same dark behavior patterns of their families and clans. Some call it tradition or a family pattern of thoughtless cruel behavior to the SELF and the children.

The darkest ones on earth are under a great deal of physical and spiritual stress and are acting out. Their dark thought and actions are being exposed. Darker souls allow demons to posses the biology creating a "regressive walk-in" that has awareness of the firsts' souls history. A dark entity or demon or unbalanced energy has thoughts, beliefs and behavior patterns that are less than 30% light. Their TRUTHS are blame, refusal to take responsibility, they lie, deny, twist the truth, and use control and manipulation on others to prove they are better and more powerful than others. Many parents have these dark behaviors with their children. When the human dissociates or is in an addictive state or the biology dies a demon can attach and control the biology.

Demon possession is the work of human imbalance supported by mythology. A demon is an entity that is 70-100% dark. So if one of your dead relatives possesses your biology at times and they are also 70-100% dark they could also be called a demon. Dark entities like to put you in fear and help you put yourself down so they can enter your biology when they like and encourage you to do what they liked to do. They want you to engage in the addictions and dark activities they enjoyed. Your awareness of them and your refusal to play their dark games make them go away to find an easier mark.

Satanic Cults have ceremonies to invite demons into their members especially the newborn that is trained to ALLOW demons in and encourage them to enter and take over the biology. Possession is a real creation by a human. What you believe you create by focusing on it. The purpose of demon possession is to give the little human super powers on this dense planet of matter and human negativity. Dark entities are your basic con artist running a con on the little human and frequently stays with the same family for generation after generation running the same con on each new generation that has receptive members. On this planet of free will you need to choose not to allow your self to dissociate or let an addiction or suffering be your excuse for leaving your biology unattended. The core personality of the abused HIDES OUT because it is overwhelmed by its very harsh experiences of allowing another to create for them.

When there is a soul aspect transfer the new aspect does not acquire the old aspects spiritual wisdom or history. The new soul aspect needs to negotiate its own experiences and higher truths. But the history of the old aspect is known and the situations the old aspect got stuck in are still present for the new aspect to deal with. They will know the facts of the old aspects history but not have the feeling, emotion or wisdom of the old aspect. The old stuck aspect watches the progress of the new aspect. The new aspect will not have the emotional trauma and fear level of the previous aspect. Walk-ins, braid-ins and blend-ins are all possible options for the new soul aspects.

ANIMAL SOULS or members of a HERD or FLOCK share unified soul pools OR there can be very individualized souls animating some of our pets. There are soul walk-ins in animals. Relationships between humans and companion animals can have elements rarely found between humans. The companion animal and human can share elements of their soul aspects and the two will work together sharing their challenges on this tough planet. Sometimes when an important person to us has lost their biology an aspect of them can enter your companion animal to continue the connection to protect and guide you. An aspect of a loving relative that transitioned could be in the family dog because they still wishes to look out for another family member.

Companion animals will often act out the emotions of its owner that have been repressed or disowned by the human. Sometimes the animal will take on symptoms and "share" an illness with the human to assist him or her. The animal may even die from the illness the human failed to grasp the spiritual significance of and heal. Animals often provide much needed unconditional love or energetic protection for the human. Animal love is unconditional and they volunteered to teach humans about compassion.

Chapter 5
GOING LIGHTER

The RAPTURE or the DAY of JUDGMENT or ASCEN-SION or May 21, 2011 marked a larger separation between those individuals moving to greater light or great dark thinking. For those moving to greater light there was a large delivery of energy increasing the gap between the dark and light. The light Beings are being more supportive and proactive taking actions of support for those moving lighter. The dark will be having babies without souls. Those with more dark than light can no longer incarnate on earth. Those that have gone light will find it more dangerous to play with the dark ones than it has been historically to play with darkness.

When you have committed to going lighter or ALIGN yourself with universal law there are many little steps taken to get there and our soul aspects keep track or measurements of each step you take toward the light or universal law. Each step out of darkness toward the light is considered one-ascension. It is possible to have hundreds of dark ascensions before getting to the half dark / half light ascension marker of you carrying 70% light consistently. Only 2% of the earth's population has had "one light ascension" or more for all of their incarnations on earth.

ASCENSION is a step-by-step marker for the human trying to realign with universal law. Give and receive only unconditional love and compassion. When you decide to move into the next lesson of ascension and master it you start the process of ascending. We are ascending WITHOUT physically dying or being born or having new childhood traumas to deal with. We are retaining our memory of our self and our darker behavior patterns NOT in alignment with universal law.

One-ascension is equal to the spiritual wisdom normally gained in one lifetime. As your ascensions continue the little human releases more duality, blaming, judgment, attachment, gossip, drama, compromise and spiritual competition. The little human strives to be sovereign. With each ascension or void we enter we grieve the LOSS of the human we thought we were or the behavior pattern that we have released. Ascension is the process of the biology, soul and astral bodies integrating. Through clearing and balancing all of our thoughts and bodies in a step-by-step manner you earn ascension. Waffling or following others puts you back into duality and out of alignment with universal law. Being humiliated or glorifying being a victim or caretaker is not a higher truth. No secrets, unethical or withholding needed information from yourself or others. Following or fearing others translates into worshiping a false god or idol instead of honoring YOU first. When you pull in ANY negativity, karma or duality back into your life you decrees the amount of light you can carry.

When your focus is on whom to blame and not WHY you failed to think for yourself you are playing in the dark cycle of victim predator. You are using regressive thinking chains. Going back to less developed psychological and emotional thought. Regressive is unconscious or blaming or letting others do your thinking for you and you having a desire for others to take responsibility for you and your happiness. You are not taking responsibility for YOUR creations. Recreate to your liking. A VICTIM is an unconscious creator. The UNAWAKENED think they are victims or predators or servants and their purpose is to suffer, kill or control or be victimized. Awakening spiritually is you knowing that YOU are a soul pretending to be human and you are the creator of your reality by default or consciously.

Playing with dark and using their rules or truths entrains all players to the low vibration of dark and being a victim and predator. It is not possible to have a win-win-win experience when you are using dark rules or behavior patterns. When you allow others to think for you or you want to "beat them at there own game" by outsmarting them you are using dark truths that fail to bring you or them any light. Dark behaves as it does because it feels betrayed, very wounded and angry about being the victim. The victim reasons that being the predator or punisher will create fairness or justice or balance for them and it never does. That is the spiritual lesson we are to master in the dark reality we live in now. Dark truths NEVER create balance. Punishing, blaming, judging or "making someone pay" never brings you light or wisdom you only get dark truths reinforced one more time.

The way to change your dark reality is to own it and put your focus on light thoughts of balance and harmony. A sugar coating on dark thought patterns is more denial. Dark ones and victims are not ethical they use deception and call it love. Spouses and children of abusers and predators frequently protect their abuser because they are entrained with each other in codependency and self hate. One side of the coin believes that no one could care about or love them unless forced and controlled to have contact with them. The other side of the same coin believes they don't deserve anything better or more compassionate because they think they are worthless and need punishment. Those beliefs are dark truths and distortions to control you. There are also those that try a short cut to take what they want or think they lack or need and kill others to get what they want.

Dark thoughts and emotion throw the biology out of balance and prevent or greatly slow its ability to rebalance itself. Your upset about anything creates stress in the biology. For example when you get angry or twisted about something it takes the biology 6 hours to rebalance itself physically, after you have calmed down emotionally. If you never calm down the stress is constant. The infant or child feels a 100 times stronger than an adult would feel in the same situation. As children when we experience trauma, which is considered an overwhelming jolt to our mind or body it works its way through our 3 astral bodies spiritual, emotional mental and lastly hits us physically. The information we are UNABLE to process during times of trauma will get stored in our muscles and bones as tension or pockets of density, that translates into being hyper vigilant, fearful or angry and in a constant state of stress that keeps the biology out of balance and in dysfunction.

The biology creates actual pockets of liquid or density in different parts of the biology when we feel reoccurring negative emotion. Your ANGER about being raped as an infant or child may be stored as a sac of clear liquid in the large intestine. Each time you get STRONGLY angered about that old wound or suffer a new trauma like that the amount of liquid in that sac increases. You may even have three pockets of anger, one for violent physical abuse, one pocket for the humans that abused you and never rescued you and one pocket for the soul aspects that failed to rescue you because you live on a planet of free will and that would be interference on their part.

Another example is a pocket of dense energy and feeling about a parent using you sexually or when the parent is lonely and then rejecting you WHEN they are done with you UNTIL they want to use you again. You are to be invisible and have NO NEEDS until they want to use you again. This particular "pocket of density" could be located next to your spine around the kidneys or adrenals. To heal or release that pocket you would need to "RELIVE" your feelings about your parent forcing, needing or seducing you and rejecting you and any needs you may have never being addressed. You would need to own your OWN personal feelings when you were that age. Own how the inner child of 3 felt when he or she was treated like that. Your job now is to have compassion and protection for the abused infant or child you were so that aspect can integrate with you now and grow up. Understanding or justifying "why" the adult involved did what they did will not help YOU release YOUR "pocket of density" at all.

When you reach a point of releasing "your anger" emotionally and mentally at your abusers and your soul aspects the pocket of density will release physically in the form of liquid or tension. That lesson of blame will be over and healed unless you pull it back again to experience another time of "justifiable anger" that goes against universal law. Discern the larger picture to release the anger.

FORGET MICROMANAGING

Allowing is acceptance of the knowledge that everything is as it ought to be and there is no need for you to micromanage anything not even yourself. The law of allowing means you allow others even when they do not allow you. As you consistently practice the law of allowing you will realize that what others think of you isn't important to you or your spiritual growth. Judging yourself against others keeps you entrained to their level of dark or light and you off your path. Allowing puts you into the universal flow of compassion. Remind yourself they are doing the best they can with their current beliefs and circumstances and NOT your needs and desires. There is freedom in allowing others to be whom and what they are. Even when the reality they created brings them poverty, war, addiction or disease allowing them to focus on their creation allows you to focus on your creation. There are many more sides or "points of perception" than yours. That allows everyone his or her own individual freedom to follow the path they want to experience and learn from. Their experiences do not need to be in alignment with what you have created for you.

Tolerating others or things means you have emotional attachment to their creations and made a negative judgment. To achieve allowing means you need to release your "desire for" and "control of" the HOW, WHEN and WHAT. The how and when is decided by your soul aspects and the synchronicities they line up. When you are impatient your focus moves to WAITING, you go darker and the law of attraction brings "more waiting" into your reality. Trust and faith in your soul aspects to bring what you need and when you need it will bring more light and enthusiasm to you. NOTICE what is brought to you and use it, experience it. Notice and follow your strong feelings. When you work with your soul, things come easier, circumstances shift and opportunities appear. Action shouldn't be painful or difficult and when it is rethink what you are thinking. It should feel right not forced. When you put limits on what you will and will not allow you are "taking control of" or forcing and not allowing.

The universal law of **ACTION** means the human must ACT first to start the ball rolling. Make the many little moves to get things started and prove your commitment to the direction you are moving in. Then your soul aspects will line up synchronicities for you in the vibration or level of compassion you function in. The universal law of allowing means no more attachment to outcomes or agendas, any judgment or blame.

We attract what we focus on and allow that to come into our reality. When you have doubt, fear, or worry and that vibration dominates that is what you create and allow into your reality. For example your "fear of lack" will attract another with low self-esteem that is looking to use someone and take what he or she can and you feel you are so worthless that is what you deserve. You have helped each other create the reality you both focused on.

The universal principle of RELATIVITY is viewing and understanding from a particular viewpoint and that is relative and accurate to the viewer's point of perception. When you do not love yourself you attract others that are dark and do not love themselves and are not trustworthy.

The universal principle of AWARENESS is for you to observe the illusion of separation that this matrix and duality present. You need to realize how much darkness there is on earth and in your reality. Are you recreating dark by giving dark judgment and blame to others? This reality is a role-playing game designed to increase your discernment and spiritual wisdom.

The universal principle of LIABILITY says we are held liable for the use, abuse or neglect of the rights we have and earned. When you allow dark to control your reality YOU have allowed the daily recreation of dark in your reality. Gathering a group together to go against what you decide is injustice in your reality goes against the law of allowing. When you do not like your reality you need to change it for you alone. That is your job to undo or release what you alone created in many lifetimes on earth with its dark bias.

The universal principle of COMPENSATION is what we genuinely think, DO and say we get the same kind or energy in return. Our soul aspects "not the human" decide how and when we are compensated. The reward is as large as you are able to NOTICE and receive graciously. Limitation comes from your refusal to see, own and use the wisdom or clue offered to you. Synchronicities, "gods gifts" or the legion of lights blessings need to be allowed in or received by YOU. Most of us have been operating with the "dark rules of survival" and staying alive. We have been raised, taught, used and controlled by dark truths. Religion and darkness have been dismal failures at teaching people to have love and compassion for the self. When you don't love yourself FIRST your ability to love anything or anyone else is drastically reduced and high vibrational gifts are not accepted or allowed into your reality.

The principle of PROSPERITY is you prosper in direct proportion to the enjoyment you receive in seeing the prosperity of yourself and others. Your prosperity is denied in direct proportion to your feelings of guilt, envy or hostility for being prosperous or witnessing other's prosperity. When one prospers all may prosper. Maintain a prosperous attitude even in states of poverty to move to prosperous states. Allowing and accepting what your thoughts have brought you means you own and incorporate the law of allowing in your world.

You cannot change any other person's world for them. When you have no desire to control others you free up your energy for you. Darkness and dark behavior does not believe in allowing anyone free choice. Dark always knows what is best for everyone else. Even the dark leaders are controlled and forced by the dark tyrants above them. You need to prioritize, service to others or compassion for you first. Caretaking and service to others first is a way to BLACKMAIL others into valuing you because you DO NOT value yourself. Anyone's opinion carries more weight than your opinion. The more you force or use another the less freedom they have to be and do what they want. The more you force or use another the less freedom YOU have to do, as you want. Allowing and wisdom gathering is mastered on an individual basis.

The parent or adult that allows a predator or abuser to have contact with a small child IS VIOLATING the child's rights. The unawakened think they are victims or predators or servants and their purpose is to suffer, kill, control or be victimized or allow their child to be victimized. Living with a dark bias on earth for so long has taught us to accept some pretty dark thoughts and behaviors as NORMAL and NATURAL. Yes they are normal and natural behavior for a low dark vibration. And it is normal and natural for those that live in the dark vibration of "power to the little human" because they believe that is all there is and they deny their soul.

The universal law of DIVINE MANIFESTATION is win-win-win-win to benefit all involved and harm to none. Any harm to another in the process or outcome of creation is not DIVINE and carries karmic debt. The principle of FREEDOM is that there is space for expansion and growth for ALL without restricting others space to grow. No one is free until each is free and all are freeing each other.

WE have NEVER been ALONE

Our perception has always been that we are here on earth alone when in fact there has been a great deal of evidence, legends and art pieces to point to the contrary that we have dismissed as fantasy or failed to link them all together. A mind-boggling amount of information has been kept from us and we are frequently lied to. Other races on other planets have always taken an active role in and on earth. We are closely watched by the beings that carry a lot of light and micromanaged and controlled by the dark beings. Different races from other planets have come to help, guide, share their DNA or control and use humans and Gaia as a natural resource.

One small example of twisting the facts is "angels flying" found in religious texts and we infer they are protecting us. The flying angles are symbolic of reptilians that have wings and can fly just like the gargoyle can fly. The gargoyle, not a creature of light, is found on illuminati homes, cathedrals, churches, and buildings like the British Houses of Parliament. Seraph stands for fiery serpent. The reptilians use us the way we use livestock.

SIRIUS is the brightest star in the sky south of the celestial equator in the constellation Canis Major. Sirians are a mixture of helpful and not so helpful people. Sirius A has many human races. They are merchants of the universe selling and TRADING technology and information but never provide technology that could be used against them. They are builders, artists, musicians and are close to nature. They are not very political. Their governments are based on spiritual technologies that use sound and color. Sirius A had a strong influence in Ancient Egypt.

Orion / Draco contributions have been dark and designed to control and use the population of earth as slaves or livestock. They are responsible for all humans having 15% or more reptilian DNA since the time of Atlantis. They have covertly controlled ever aspect of the way we function politically, financially and socially. They have dumbed us down with the foods and illnesses they have forced on us as a planet.

Aliens and extraterrestrials have visited Earth throughout Gaia's history and have left many large settlements, their descendants and beliefs. On the lighter side the ANDROMEDAN COUNCIL has 139 different races represented to facilitate evolution of all civilizations in the Milky Way Galaxy by mentoring them. On earth they are working to fill in all the knowledge we lack about our history and helping the dark ones to release their hold on humans and all our institutions.

The Galactic Federation is monitoring our movement to greater light and helping when they can. By divine dispensation they will put a stop to weapons of mass destruction and ensure that there will be safe places on earth to live in peace and create enlightened communities. Our recorded history is chock full of lies, mysteries and unexplained events that our controllers know the answers to and much more.

The ORION or GALACTIC WARS have been fought in the Milky Way Galaxy engulfing large parts of it for more than 20 million years with no breakthroughs by either side for long. The Anchara Alliance was mostly Reptilian Races that originally came from another universe when it was blended with our own. They were more aggressive, lacked emotion and had the conviction that they had a god given right to have dominance over the entire Milky Way Galaxy. The wars started over territory in the constellation of Lyra and spread to Orion becoming a war of beliefs.

Initially the philosophy of service to self was similar to communism that implied everybody takes care of them self, which is an excellent philosophy in higher vibrations but in lower dark vibrations of duality it always turns into the predator and victim cycle of fear and force.

Four million years ago the victims and their allies joined forces against the Alliance of Anchara to protect themselves. The Galactic Federation represents over a thousand star systems in this region of our galaxy. The Alliance of Anchara agreed to relinquish its claims to Earth in 1995 with the TREATY of ANCHARA and the Galactic federation ending the galactic wars. The Annunaki switched sides to the Galactic Federation. Some of the dark side middle management, the illuminati is not letting go so that is why we still have the ill affects of the dark on earth.

Patterns of darkness are the same all over the universe. The individual wants MORE power, fame or stuff. They want to be worshipped and followed but settle for another fearing them. They can't be trusted and do not keep their word. All these behaviors are the way people behave when they have little or no compassion for them self because they do not feel worthy.

Darkness in any individual on any planet has an inability to feel compassion for others. We need compassion for our wounds, our physical, emotional and spiritual wounds of betrayal, misuse and abuse. Dark is predictable, self destructive, angry and frustrated because they do not think they are worthy of love and compassion. They have been wounded and adopted the "dark belief" of not being worthy. To heal the wound you must own it and know because you breathe you are good enough to have compassion for you.

All our issues, wounds and pretty lies about what was true are coming into our awareness to heal. There is a "point of separation" suspended in space or your "inner child" at the age you first received that wound. The same kind of wound received over and over again will be in loops and bundled together. For example all the times your parent betrayed you. When you can move to the first wounding event on this chain of same or similar events, own and embrace those experiences they will heal. Own your true feelings and anything you may have told yourself like a word or phrase about your experience to release it.

Your soul aspect can give you a slide show of the event and what your thoughts were. That experience has spiritual wisdom for you. Gather the wisdom to release the "emotion charge" and the reason "you think you are unworthy." The inner child will be the age of the first event. After you heal the wound integrate the child into you and promise to protect and care for the wounded child from now on.

The amount of light you carry reflects your dark and light MORAL choices. The percentages of light or dark choices you make are clear indications of your personality type, the band of vibration you function in and what you will and won't do, generally speaking. What you currently experience in life will be what you will continue to experience because the laws of attraction, entrainment and you allowing it will create more of the same in your future. Changing your thought in one direction or another will create something different for you. I use the words "light" "light gray" "dark," "dark gray" and "black" to represent the amount of light the little human carries.

BLACK or DARK or close to 100% IMBALANCED with no light. They are dangerous to be with or trust. They are negative, self-hating, unconsciousness, narcissistic or dissociated. They use other humans, children and animals like objects or things. Around 15% of them on earth are soulless.

DARK GRAY or VERY IMBALANCED has less than 30% light. They emanate, attract and reflect darkness. Are likely to be possessed by a dark ancestor some of the time. The amount of dark the ancestor has will emanate from them during possession and that will be the amount of light they carry at those times. When they have multiples personalities or DID Dissociative Identity Disorder each personality will carry its own amount of light that is reflected in that personality or alter. Their feelings and emotions are resentment, anger, antagonism, blame, acting out, self-abuse, addiction and living life in anxiety and fear. They operate by abandoning their biology and awareness. To deal with their suffering they shut off their feelings and senses.

A LIGHTER GRAY carries 30% to 60% light and they are in and out of awareness functioning in fear, boredom or indifference most of the time. Their personality is being oppositional, angry and in pain. They are self-absorbed, gossipy, frequently leave their biology and live in past time and old wounds and irrational much of the time. They twist facts to defend their dark, often cruel reality. The largest area of seduction and darkness for the biology or ego or the little human or the dark soul aspect is SEXUAL. Dark entities use sex to control, manipulate and steal energy.

LIGHT GRAY entities that are fully conscious carry 60% to 80% light. They function in awareness, interest, eagerness and creativity. With 70% light an entity or demon cannot posses your biology because you won't let it. You are having compassion for yourself.

Each group helping us now has various shades of gray and individuals in each group are various shades of gray. Always you need to discern the amount of light in others you put your trust in.

Chapter 6
FREE WILL / CHOICE

In the beginning there was the legion of light, which are quanta of light. Then there was SOUND and its vibration. Electron motion creates heat and magnetism or universal unconditional love. The magnetic motion creates light, sound and color. The sound, color and light create VERY PERDICTABLE patterns that we call sacred geometry. One rule of the earth role-playing game is we all get FREE WILL. That means the human gets to choose WHEN, HOW, WHY and WHERE they want to learn a lesson or balance their energy. The WHAT lesson is to be mastered was decided or determined before your birth. Whatever aspect of your spiritual wisdom is most out of balance needs to be addressed first. It is all-sacred geometric patterns of behavior the dark are too unconscious to see or feel. That is why they are dangerous to play with or have as a parent, spouse or friend.

Free will is only found in lower vibrational worlds or the 3rd and 4th dimensions. On earth we got so dark and out of balance we forgot that we do not need to accept the limits and controls that dark people set. We did not remember we could escape by aligning with universal law. Dark encourages you to feel worthless and guilty keeping your vibration low and slow.

Time is circular or in cycles. History repeats itself in cycles to afford us another chance over and over again to master the lesson we came to earth to master and balance our energy. We came to study how the dark negative behavior tears down our self worth and confidence. Hate is blocked love with a DEEP wish to be loved and accepted by the one you hate, even when it is yourself. When intense hate is your focus the law of attraction will bring more hate until you change your focus. Hate is blaming someone or thing for not giving you what you WANTED. Now you need to give it to your self.

To end something you want to stop doing, stop taking action. That is what the young are helping us do by breaking the old structured systems of control and force. They are not doing things the way they have always been done. The way to stop war is to stop being a participant in it. If you don't show up there can't be a war or fight. The young are waiting and not participating. Our ways of functioning have maintained the dark bias on earth for thousands of years. There are higher vibrational patterns to master in present time. Our economy has gotten stuck. Unemployment breaks down our slavery to STUFF and stops us long enough to move in another direction. Politics and politicians deceptions are being brought to light and they are being prosecuted. Transparency is happening in every facet of our life.

We are in a 200-year cycle of transitioning that started in the 1940s and 1950s. During this cycle we need to channel light and compassion individually. Being in a group will not get you to higher vibrations. The time is over for dark negativity and groups forcing agendas it is against the law of allowing. To rejoin higher vibration and compassionate living we need to each do it individually. The universal law of FREE WILL is divine will granting each entity the right to direct and pursue his or her life so long as he or she does not violate the same right of others. A right that excludes the rights of others is NOT divine. Free will is found in lower vibrational worlds or dimensions as a tool for instruction about the way dark functions and how easy it is to get sucked into their back and forth game of force and control.

SEARCH for SELF-VALUE There are people that control others with their money because they feel worthless. Their money makes them feel they can force or buy love or self worth with their money.

There are people that control others with their LACK of money because they feel worthless. Their "money lack" puts them in a position of needing to be taken care of which they translate into being worth something and having some value.

Both groups of people are playing the same game. I NEED someone or thing outside of me to prove I have value or worth so I can feel somewhat loved or valued. The feeling never lasts and they are always looking for more and more external approval. The search for external approval and compassion means you are still playing in the low vibrational CYCLE of VICTIM and PREDATOR. The victim is an unconscious creator. The UNAWAKENED think they are victims or predators or servants and their purpose is to suffer, kill or control or be victimized. Awakening spiritually is you knowing that YOU are a soul pretending to be human and you ARE the creator of your reality and your experiences.

Dark's creations always end up being a form of the victim predator cycle. Playing with dark and using their rules entrains all players to the low vibration of dark and being a victim or the predator. It is not possible to have a win-win-win experience when you are using dark rules or behavior patterns. When you allow others to think for you or you want to "beat them at there own game" by outsmarting them you are using dark truths that fail to bring you or them any light. Dark behaves as it does because it feels betrayed, very wounded and angry about being the victim. The victim reasons that being the predator or punisher will create fairness or justice or balance for them and it never does. That is the spiritual lesson we are to master in the dark reality we live in now. Dark truths NEVER create balance or self-love. Punishing, blaming, judging or "making someone pay" never brings you light or wisdom you only get dark truths reinforced one more time or the serpent eating its own tail.

Is dark in denial about the vibration they are sending out that triggers the law of attraction to bring them more of what they have. Using dark truths will always bring more darkness, because that is the reality the dark one vibrates, projects and maintains. Darkness is what they create and it becomes their reality. The way to change a dark reality is to own it and put your focus on light thoughts of balance, harmony and compassion for you first. A sugar coating is more denial. Dark ones and victims are not ethical they use force and deception that they call being loving.

You are not the victim because your vibration called for more darkness. Gaia historically had emanated darkness attracting other dark ones. Earth's population is 71% dark in 2011 reflecting the light Gaia USED to carry. Spouses and children of abusers and predators frequently protect their abuser because they are entrained with each other in the low vibration of codependency and self hate. One side of the coin believes that no one could care about or love them unless forced and controlled to have contact with them. The other side of the same coin believes they don't deserve anything better or more compassionate because they think they are worthless and need punishment. Those beliefs are dark truths and distortions designed to control you. Some kill to take what they want or think they lack or need. They are looking for self-love in all the wrong places.

INDIVIDUAL MIND or GROUP MIND

The individual and the group mind play off each other and serve to inspire and suppress each other. They are always linked and interactive for each individual and the group. The group and individual enrich and support each other when balanced. Playing off each other increases individual and group creativity and options when aligned with universal law. Our mental body is aware of the others in our various groups and maintains the connections. For example the biologies on earth are in need of more nutritious food. Balance of the individual contribution to the group and the group focus and support create win-win-win situations.

Frequently we surrender individual thought and responsibility when we join a group. This is most common in lower vibrations. "Group think" or do what the leader says is a tool used by the dark to control others. Wisdom and allowing can only be learned and mastered individually. GROUPTHINK is a psychological phenomenon that occurs within groups. Group members try to minimize conflict and reach a consensus without critically evaluating different ideas or viewpoints because there is only one viewpoint. The "point of view" from the top bully that works its way down to the bottom level. This process acts like a hive, an army, a cult or dysfunctional family or robots and all do what they are told, and there is no individual creativity or input. That results in irrational and dehumanizing actions against some members in the group and any group they attack. Our military is trained to groupthink and dehumanize the enemy so it is easier to kill them.

GROUP MIND or COLLECTIVE CONSCIOUSNESS is the thought, feeling and actions of each individual group member COMBINED into one thought and feeling representing the group. Collectives develop a sense of oneness and teamwork among each member like a country or town does. Usually group mind occurs within a certain physical location for a spiritual purpose. Each member has access to the combined knowledge and experiences of all its members to work with and build on. They share the thoughts, fears, hopes, and desires of the inhabitants. Each galaxy has a group mind or living energy field that is the sum of all the SPECIES present in the collective consciousness. For example the earth emanated a magnetic field creating an attraction to darkness and the victim predator cycle.

The DNA or genetic code is embedded in the galactic mind and emanates from its magnetic field creating an attraction. There are planetary minds with a living energy field and solar system minds and universal minds. The loops of similar events and the souls of Lemuria and Atlantis are back on earth in present time or concurrently to see if we can raise the group consciousness. As individuals from that group start aligning with universal law they bring the group vibration up from the "dark group mindset" changing outcomes. As one mind-controlled slave awakens and changes they will help other slaves awaken to move from robotic control to THINKING for the self and aligning with universal law. The illuminati had targeted the turn of the century to have their COVERT control of humans to become OVERT with the New World Order and New World Religion.

The energy of the group mindset can attach itself to physical objects like buildings, statues, rocks, and bodies of water and a planet that store energy. The group mind phenomenon is different from mob or "out of control" groups.

Each group has a GROUP SOUL that is the collective spiritual essence of a community, nation, or ethnic group. The group soul provides guidance and focus for the group purpose. When the group gets imbalanced it creates its own karma like the Jewish, Mormon, Catholic and Nazi groups have done. The process goes like this; individuals within the group have dark or negative purposes of force and control. Others in the group go along with it and the group gets darker and darker. The dark ones give a lie or deception and the follower's stop thinking for themselves and own the lie. Those buying the lie serve and support the dark agenda and the group gets darker and darker because those NOT buying the lie leave the group. The light ones leave to allow the dark their path and darker ones are attracted and join.

The group soul is created with the birth of the group, strengthens and weakens to reflect the direction of the group and dies when the group disbands or merges with another group.

GROUP INCARNATIONS happen when a higher vibrating group wants to assist a lower vibrational group. Then you have volunteers that come into biology together as a group to support and help increase spiritual awareness through example as a group with a shared goal. During any civilization that evolved faster than the rest of earth civilizations there was a group incarnation of volunteers for example the golden ages of the Roman Empire, Egypt and Greece. Some group incarnations challenged the political, economic and religious DOGMA and unconsciousness of the time. Group incarnations are an attempt to wake people up so they can think for them self.

The volunteers were NOT perfect and were subjected to the same dark pressures of living on earth the rest of us suffer. Many got darker and darker. The edge the group incarnation HAS; is the higher vibration to start out with and they generally stay in close contact with their soul aspects that gave them information and support when they asked for it because this is a planet of free will.

WISDOM is mastered individually. Through your interactions with others in the group you learn how wise you are personally. How large a bully you are or how supportive and nurturing you are. Your personal wisdom is relative to the reality or situation you are in. Wisdom is the knowledge you have accumulated from ALL your experiences on Gaia with and without biology. ALLOWING is done individually all day every day.

BRAINWAVES or DIMENSIONS

Our body is a biological computer and our feelings or emotions change the atoms and sub-atomic particles to literally alter our physical reality. When you change the subatomic particles we consist of emotionally you restructure your matter or biology. We are our reality so we can't imagine a reality that exists without us because the act of OBSERVING our self restructures us. What we expect to observe will be there because we created it on a subatomic level. Consciousness comes through us and emanates from us. Consciousness is the programming language of our world or universe. The unconscious use limited and corrupted programs.

When you switch OFF your brain and mental body to HOOKUP your consciousness into our mainstream media or illusion you get manipulated in the direction the media WANTS to take you. Your goals and aspirations become what advertisers want from you. Someone else is in charge of your consciousness. Our parents, religions and leader of your country take control of your consciousness when you do not. You become the unconscious victim to the demands of mainstream media or your spouse and their rules and regulations. You adopt an EX-TERNAL creation of reality for your self.

When you are aware and communicating with your soul aspect. You are using YOUR programming language to increase your vibration. 5th dimension is not a hologram like 3rd and 4th dimension. Holographic realities are places of learning for as long as it takes you to incorporate universal law as your truth. Fifth dimension is a reality where you integrate all you learned in the lower vibrational worlds. When our thoughts and emotions become fearful it lowers our awareness and vibration this is simply a matter of resonance and not punishment. Our reality is a result of our vibration or alignment or lack of alignment with universal law.

DIMENSIONS do not occupy time or space because they are consciousness and each dimension has a FIXED vibration or awareness. Dimensions have different THEMES or purposes with different vibrations that all interact with each other. They can move and shift like our thoughts do. Dimensions are distinct event sites and there are infinite numbers of sites and particular planes of consciousness or spiritual light. The first three universal wholes, 1st, 2nd and 3rd dimension are given order by the 4th dimension of time. The universal whole is a self-created, self-sustaining MENTAL creation or holograph.

When we were last functioning in the 6th dimension our essence or soul aspect chose the form or biology we have in matter at this time here on earth. The soul chooses what particular planet, galaxy and dimension it wanted to inhabit. Those picking earth were interested in understanding how seductive and all consuming dark truths are. While in the 6th dimension we created our blueprint or "patterns of behaviors," or beliefs or the "psychological issues we wanted to address" to test our moral fiber. This reality was designed to be experienced in the 4th dimension. Things got darker and darker until we all wound up in the 3rd dimension. Darkness happens. When the little human kept making darker and darker choices the dark belief or pattern gets stuck and the biology easily becomes diseased or unbalanced.

How some different dimensions or vibrations work in us, FIRST and SECOND DIMENSIONS are quantum realities, too small to see. Our instinct or innate knowledge is a 2nd dimensional ability to tune into the planet and know where there is water and food that will heal us or poison us. Know when a predator is stalking or simply sharing our space. Instincts are usually sensory awareness that our left-brain, logical self has been trained to ignore. Some religions want you to think it is the devil. The body's instincts pull together information from our senses just below our conscious perception. When the distant vision, quiet sound, faint odor, proximity of someone or something we cannot touch comes together in our right brain we get the meaning of the subliminal information. INTUITION is similar to instinct with the addition of information from our soul aspects or the invisible realm.

Empathy is another 2nd dimensional perception when you pay attention to it. Empathy can become a problematic sensation when we fail to differentiate between what is our feeling and what is another's feeling. Empathy is not limited to time and space and we can feel an emotion from someone far away and someone not having biology.

Fear and anger are very loud emotions to activate the survival response of fight or flight you are in life and death danger. Anger's purpose is to break through barriers. Sadness is not as loud but is very contagious it creates bonding, sympathy and care taking.

Happiness urges procreation of the species.

When our consciousness expands from the 1st dimension of quantum reality through to the 5th dimension we gain freedom from time and space. 4th and 5th dimensional skills are precognition or seeing the future in the now moment. The lower 4th dimension is often labeled Hell and is a realm of fear and darkness. Hell is not a place. It is a resonance of the lower 4th dimension. The 4th dimension is the aura of planet earth and the aura of each person. Be aware that because a person is "dead" and speaking from the 4th dimension does not mean that they know more than they did when they were alive in the 3rd dimension. They will misdirect you in the same ways they did when they were alive. Messages from the fifth dimension and beyond come into our awareness in a flash of light without negativity. Frequently they are a package of awareness with pictures.

Our aura filters our perceptions of our reality. When our filter is darkened with fear or negativity our expanded perceptions will be darkened too. To heal our self is to heal our aura so we can differentiate between messages from the lower astral plane or the 4th dimension and messages from higher vibrations and our higher vibrating soul aspect.

The universe is made up of unconditional compassion or photons. Our thoughts organize the quanta of the universe into the creations our thought.

The PINEAL GLAND is located in the middle of the head and balances both the left and right hemispheres of the brain helping them work together. The pineal gland is a stargate or portal built into our biology. The pineal gland controls the physical and nonphysical world and balances the LIQUIDS in humans. Water is energy and is in evolution now. During the transition or great shift humans will carry more water for a bit to acclimate to higher vibrations and then less water when the biology becomes more crystalline and our light increases. Our pineal gland receives photon energy into the biology. The little human reality resides in the left side of the brain. Multidimensions reside in the right hemisphere and those two are being reconnected now.

As the biology changes and adjusts so will your eating change and then change again. Some days you may not be able to eat anything and other days you can't get enough to eat. You may crave foods that are unusual for you. You may find that you have developed intolerance or allergy to wheat and dairy. Learn to listen to and trust your biology, being flexible in your eating habits is essential.

Our sleep patterns are variable so it is wise to adjust your belief system about how much sleep is needed to feel good and that will change. You may not be able to sleep but cannot get up either. Naps become important to some and very refreshing when the body is changing so fast.

Our senses are increasing and expanding. Sounds are louder or grating and become intolerable. Smell becomes acute and you can smell fear. Your skin or touch gets so sensitive you can no longer wear clothes made of synthetics, natural fiber clothing like cotton, silk, bamboo or hemp clothing feel better on your skin. Many are experiencing electrical surges throughout their biology, which can cause some dizziness or feeling of lost balance for a few seconds to a few minutes. These shifts are the realignment of our reality.

Chapter 7
DARK CHOICES and 3rd DIMENSION

We were in the 4th dimension making too many dark choices individually and then as a group. The group fell into a lower vibration and the 3rd dimension. What you create individually and as a group you need to uncreate individually and as a group. The wisdom comes when you KNOW why you created what you have and the tweaks and adjusting needed to create more compassion and equality for all.

THIRD DIMENSION is based on and created with multiple lies, illusion and secrets. Lies about what is real and about who you are. That is how darkness and unconsciousness ALWAYS operates. To move out of 3rd and 4th dimension, duality and separation the lies and YOUR self deceptions need to be exposed, owned and the "emotional charge" or suffering as a result of the deceptions and lies need to be released.

We planned our experiences for the 4th dimension and made so many little dark choices we wound up in the 3rd dimension. Morally we experienced the split of dark and light or YOU and ME and "free will." We created a holographic illusion SUSTAINED with our thoughts and perceptions of separation, opposites, linear time, death and forgetting. Suffering allows awareness of going against universal law. Our biology allowed our soul aspect to experience 3rd dimension in the "schoolroom earth. When we calibrate our consciousness to Beta brainwaves the primary experience is the third dimension and below. Reality is perceived as OUTSIDE of you and you feel you are separate. The little human core belief is that it is a victim. Gaia left the 3rd dimension to move into the 4th dimension in 2001. Humans are welcome to join her or not.

ALPHA and BETA brainwaves are 3rd dimensional vibrational or calibrations.

ALPHA waves are the normal relaxed brain activity. The wave frequency is 8 to 13 hertz or cycles per second. In an Alpha state you perceive both the "outside world" and "your inside world" simultaneously and you can choose to experience the collective consciousness of your group or society or mass media.

In illuminati ALPHA programming the alpha state is the easiest brain wave to reach and includes the youngest and easiest alters for handlers and trainers to reach. Infants and children that normally live in alpha states and need "training (drugging, physical trauma and electric shock)" to enter other brain waves for long periods of time to serve the illuminati agendas. There are many "systems of alters" installed and "access codes" created for handlers and trainers to use in the alpha state. Different alternate personalities are installed in the child to service adults sexually using Alpha states and may be coded as RED in some alter systems. Alpha is considered the foundation for all other programs of illuminati slaves that are installed in the very young child. In the alpha state trainers program in how to torture, use espionage, increase visual acuity and develop photographic memory.

The criminals and angry ones in our society come from three different groups. The abusive or dysfunctional parent creates one group and is not members of the illuminati. Illuminati slaves have assignments that are crimes against humans and the state all the time. There is a third group that have broken or crashed programs or just malfunction.

BETA brainwaves have 12 to 30 hertz or cycles per second and are the 2nd easiest brain wave to reach. In beta vibration your reality is perceived, as "outside" of you and you feel separated, the concept of "them" and "us" or me. The core belief would be that you are a victim or recipient of things, events and those individuals outside of you. The belief that everything good or bad comes from outside of you would make you want to PLEASE your environment to get the best outcome for your self.

Beta brainwaves are associated with aggression, survival and sexual impulses. In the illuminati the beta programming holds cult protectors, internal warriors and military systems and may be coded BLUE.

ALL the children in the illuminati are "trained sex slaves" from birth and at 2 years are programmed to have charisma and be seductive. Beta alters are used as Black Widows for espionage and blackmail. Trainers and programmers can put almost any kind of body to use as a sex slave in the crime syndicate, pornography, movies and Internet porn. Some snuff films are of having one's head chopped off while having sex or aborting a fetus. Early sexual abuse events are used or created to anchor Beta programming and alters. Beta altars generally see themselves as cats. The "scorpion vibration" was programmed for the government into the "Monarch sex slaves" both male and female sex slaves.

The BETA model can ONLY have sex with ones their handlers allows them to have sex with. They cannot refuse sexually servicing another. Slaves are constantly belittled and humiliated. Illuminati children are available to be used sexually around the world as "party favors" and for blackmail.

The sexually addicted dysfunctional parent not raised in the illuminati will create a sexually addicted child with DID, Dissociative Identity Disorder that has at least two personalities a seductive aspect and an aspect that is mean and nasty. The sexually addicted dysfunctional parent may also create children with Borderline Personality Disorder.

The FOURTH DIMENSION is more complete than the 3rd dimension and not as dense. The shifts are subtler and an energy in our awareness. Gaia and many humans (not all), cetaceans, animals, plants and the mineral kingdom are raising their consciousness and moved to 4th dimension in 2001. 4th dimension has duality and is the emotional aura of Gaia and each person. Once you expand your awareness to the 4th dimension you have memories, dreams and experiences of your parallel realities or concurrent lifetimes.

4th dimension is divided into 3 levels with entities having various agendas from outright interference with our development to assistance and blessings. We must discern which is which.

Fear and darkness are present in the lower 4th dimension and that creates a kind of "static" making it difficult for us to receive messages from higher vibrations. **HELL** is not a place. It is a resonance of the lower 4th dimension. Just as we have dark and light patches in our aura so does Gaia. There are dense places of injustice, cruelty, fear and anger that we on earth have experienced and created. There are earthbound ghosts and souls still addicted to substance, the illusion of power or justice and sexual abuse. The lost gray ones are filled with despair and hopelessness. Lower astral beings can and do SUCK energy from humans. The gray ones can possess the human and encourage them to do some pretty nasty things and they like to encourage the human to hate them self.

Some humans work on raising the vibration of these individuals by increasing their awareness THEN they can move them into a portal of greater light. The dark ones need someone lighter to help him or her "go to greater light" or "cross over" or go to the "bridge of flowers" because dark repels light. A legion of dark left the near realms on July 29, 2011 raising Gaia's light 1% from 42% to 43%.

The MIDDLE ASTRAL level of the 4th dimension is a higher vibration and some very high vibrating beings are waiting there to help us. In the middle vibration we transmute and resolve issues and density that we had in the 3rd dimension. To transmute and resolve the little human needs the ability to RE-FLECT on and have awareness of their own thoughts OR they will remain stuck and unconscious in lower vibrations.

The HIGHER ASTRAL level of the 4th dimension is beautiful and close to the fifth dimension there are many guides and teachers with information for us. In between 4th and 5th dimension is the Great Void. Dimensions one through four are on the physical/astral side of the Great Void and 5th to 8th dimensions are on the spiritual side of the Void and we gain freedom from time and space. The fourth dimension represents physical Earth's Aura/Dreamworld.

VOID or SPIRITUAL DEPRESSION

The GREAT VOID or SPIRITUAL DEPRESSION or black hole or passageway or gateway goes into all possible realities and every reality. Spiritual depression happens when your soul aspects see the human has aligned with universal law enough and is carrying 80% light and the human is ready to start the melding process with their soul aspect. The human is taken to zero point energy. That feels like numbness or being abandoned by your soul aspects. This is the leap of faith the human makes to reconnect with your soul aspects to work together as one unit.

People and things go away that are no longer a vibrational match to YOUR vibration and you move into an interdimensional state to see things through your souls point of perception. You are not falling apart you are being restructured and put back together. When the human REJECTS the spiritual depression they slip into a human depression. Your spiritual depression has been building up for many lifetimes and is part of the ascension process. The first time we have ascended and kept our biology. The cleansing tears and stories come tumbling out. You are dying and grieving your old self and releasing your limiting human story this process generally lasts a year. During that time you will slip in and out of the void and different dimensions.

Dimensions 1 to 4 are on the physical or astral side of the Great Void and dimensions 5 to 8 are on the spiritual side of the void. Realities are in the 5th to 7th dimensions and prepare you for infinite experiences as a group consciousness of the 8 to 12th dimensions. Before you can enter the fifth dimension, you must journey through the nothingness of the Great Void to fully release the illusions, limitations and separation of the polarities of duality. This can happen many times especially if you remain attached to people and things of low vibration.

The void or emptiness you feel is the sensory perceptions you experience when you move from the usual and customary for YOU to an empty aloneness. Like looking at a space you just moved out of and know you won't be going back to that space. There is an expansion of energy and you realize a belief you always operated with is NOT true at a higher vibration and you need to release it.

You are in the void or space between releasing old and adopting new truths. When beliefs crumble there is a great deal of grieving, HURT, pain and JOY that can be experienced during this process. Grieve the changes and any lose you might have. Cut cords to relationships no longer serving you. Give back any darkness you have carried for others as a child and especially from family members. Something new will come into your awareness. MENTAL and EMOTIONAL processing and transmuting are going on continuously. Generally voids last a few months or weeks. We go into the voids many times this is not a one-time event.

Another interesting phenomenon that happens in higher vibrations from the upper 4th dimension and higher is that many issues and problems go away. With each incremental rise of vibration on earth there is greater transparency and increased awareness in all areas of our existence. We get smarter. Denial, secrets, addictions or compulsions and the times you dissociate are being brought into sharp focus now so you can own your UNCON-SCIOUS creating. With the increased awareness we are SEEING things we NEVER saw before in the self in friends and in the family and our existence. There are new ways to view our leaders in business, religions, the country and the world. A constructive plan of action is easy when there is nothing hidden and no hidden agendas to second-guess at. In the higher vibrations there is no denial or secrets or dissociation from the self or others.

Denial, addictions, compulsions and secrets are used as an excuse to justify our cruel thoughtlessness to our self and others. We say to the self that it is all right to be insensitive and or demeaning to another because they are stupid or ugly or a different race or younger. The cruel thoughtless things we do are not pretty or nice they are darkness feeding off darkness. We covered up OUR awareness of our dark thoughts because we didn't like or approve of the thoughts and especially our self. It is time to own the damage denial; secrets and dissociation we cause for our self and the group we live in.

DENIAL is NEVER a strength or asset. Denial is a choice to HIDE other choices and avoid your feelings. Judgment is a form of denial. When you narrow your focus small enough to judge only an aspect of someone or something you avoid knowing about what you do not want to know or feel about your SELF. You avoid focus on your inability to be compassionate and loving to YOU. The greater your need is to deny or dissociate the more distorted and twisted things get for you.

Own what you deny so you have control over it or nothing will change. Denial and dissociation are in reality CONDONING the behavior. The higher vibration on earth since December 2009 has interfered with our ability to deny. Even when we try to deny what we know it is still "in your face" or your awareness.

When we WITHHOLD instead of REACHING "we withdraw" and we withhold information from our self and withhold compassion from the self. When you have done the least good or the most harm or injured another with a sin of omission or commission you will withhold that information if you can. A withhold is also a secret. The love you withhold from your self or others is equal to the pain you carry. Withholding love creates perpetual disintegration and drains the life force out of your intent and you. A withhold is an unspoken transgression against your moral code. If revealed the information might tarnish your self-image or put you in a position of danger or in a position to be rejected by others and your self.

With all the freedoms and increased awareness we have there are also more responsibilities on us to create win-win-win for all involved in any interaction we have.

The universal principle of **AUTHORITY** is the one aware, worthy and capable of accepting the responsibility for an act has the authority to act, initiate and accept responsibility for the act. Many want authority but will not take the responsibility for their action.

The universal principle of **RESPONSIBILITY** is when you have the ability to respond to the needs of others you receive energy from all those you respond to. This is not stealing energy but creating energy together synergistically.

The universal principle of **PENETRATION** is anything that is seen with great attention and quality of awareness penetrates the heart, which emanates into all of consciousness.

As our vibration increases any dissociation, addictions or compulsions we have will be affected. To escape reality we have also created secrets, denial and withholds. Rather than take responsibility for the experiences we created for ourselves we avoid awareness, blame others, keep secrets and deny being responsible for ourselves. Drugs to suppress anger will no longer work the way they once did. You will be aware of how your words and actions affect others. Blaming another will no longer work as an excuse for you not being responsible for you. There is no more putting things off until later or pretending you are confused and do not understand what is happening. Your denial will increase your pain and acting out until you address the dark things in your existence one way or another.

5Th **DIMENSION or THETA brainwaves**

The FIFTH DIMENSION is balancing light and dark into oneness or a whole. Anything or one, that carries a resonance lower than the fifth dimension (like a dark family member) or a "dark pattern of behavior" such as blame or being a victim that you are ATTACHED to and cannot release will keep you earth-bound and in the 3rd dimension. When you hold lower dark vibrations it is difficult to experience more than one reality at a time. Attachment will diminish your ability to stay in higher vibrations. In the 5th there is awareness of 1st to 4th dimensions. It takes patience and constant self-observation to monitor and correct the self.

In the 5th dimension light travels faster increasing harmonic resonance and colors from 72 to 123 different colors to help activate our genetic restructuring and higher vibrational skills. Integration of both brain hemispheres of our brain and sensory awareness from our mental body allows us to instantly accept, integrate and understand information from our soul aspects. Brain capacity expands from the normally used 10% in the 3rd dimension to greater awareness. Any higher vibrational awareness can enter our awareness as we can enter their awareness. We can experience any frequency of reality or dimension by calibrating our frequency to theirs. From the mid-fifth dimensions and up we sense our connection with others.

In 5th and 6th dimensions we start to merge the opposites of light and dark as we alter any unconscious thoughts we still have and align them with universal law. Any "dark pattern" we keep repeating in lower vibrations needs a new point of perception to change. We need to see the larger picture. For example when we have committed to stop blaming and start OWNING our unpleasant experiences as our own creation, then the soul aspect can rewrite and change all the old experiences of "us blaming others" in all our concurrent lifetimes. For example when we have committed to stop being the victim and own our "victimhood creations" and understand how we created what we have the soul aspect can rewrite and change all the old experiences of "us being the victim" in all our concurrent lifetimes.

THETA brainwaves are of 4 to 7 hertz or cycles per second. When your awareness is calibrated to the 5th and 6th dimension you function in THETA vibrational waves. In theta waves you experience only your "inside world" with an awareness of your biology and with practice, you are able to connect to the awareness of Gaia and her essences and experiences.

Our biology lags behind our thoughts but once your biology has recalibrated to and projects 5th and 6th dimension you can experience YOU and your interactions with your external reality. You can see and understand how you create your reality minute by minute with your beliefs. In the theta wave you desire to spend your time doing what gives you joy and stimulates your creativity. With the opening of your crown chakra sleep cycles change again and you need much more sleep, or less sleep. Your circadian cycles of wakefulness and sleep are shifting due to the constant stimulation of your pineal gland. You may also find that your dreams and meditations are move vivid and illumined than they have ever been before.

THETA programming for mind-controlled slaves is PSYCHIC warfare programming. The illuminati train their slaves to use their psychic powers to kill someone psychically from a distance by putting holes in their aura. There are even weapon systems that operate with the power of the mind and whose lethal capacity has already been demonstrated. Many of our military are young men and women of the Illuminati. Some have been seen at NORAD, in Colorado, which helps confirm that Theta models are being employed to bring in the Anti-Christ, Satan or the reptilian "large white dragon with blue eyes" or "El" the god Saturn and supreme deity represented by a black cube.

The SIXTH DIMENSION holds the blueprint or design or matrix that is projected into lower dimensions or vibrations. In the 6th dimension we write and re-write our life plans, our past experiences and patterns including releasing patterns not aligned with universal law. In the 6th dimension you are pure consciousness and choose to have a body or not have one. The sixth dimension has all possible realities and is calibrated to that vibration. You can design and create all possible realities.

PURE CONSCIOUSNESS is non-physical. They are multidimensional beings like Devas, Gods, Angels, and Archangels who exist primarily as pure consciousness and easily traverse the dimensions in service of others. These beings are able to create any form in any dimension and then return to pure consciousness with no effort. They may even choose to "wear" a human form when they feel it is the best way to be of service. Mostly they channel their resonance through those who are already physical.

DELTA waves or when the electrical activity in the brain is 0 to 8 Hertz is typical of a sleep state. Calibrated with delta cycles you ONLY experience your inside world or spiritual awareness or soul aspect with little connection to the biology. You are also able to experience Galactic awareness and are primarily attached to your higher dimensional bodies as you travel the Universe as your essence.

DELTA programming may be configured inside the illuminati child like a computer is configured with NO EMOTION and photographic memories. The Delta program has up to three levels of training and is often highly dissociated. Delta may be the "ruling" or controlling state over the other brain wave systems. Within this system are self-destruct or suicide programs, PSYCHOTIC or shatter programs and self-punishment programming. In the delta state the child can and does kill, is a bodyguard or does hostage extractions. These sequences are in delta brain wave to prevent outside access or internal access to the system. It may be color coded in orange, blue or purple and is the entry way to higher systems as jewel programming or internal councils inside the child.

The illuminati train around 10% of their children especially those that have a parent with some psychic skill. These toddlers are taught to go into Delta state and start work for the illuminati at 2 or 3 years of age to read other peoples minds and the universe to report back to their handlers what they learn. The child and adult will read other cult members, governments, planets, and solar systems, feel them and read their awareness of what is happening to keep tabs on them and control of everything going on in the universe and earth.

Once you have entered 5th dimensional realities all the time and duality is gone it is an easier transition into higher vibrations of oneness beyond the 5th and 6th dimensions. The reality you choose to perceive is the reality you are living. If you are a mind-controlled slave you are in a hypnotic or dissociated state and surrendered your freedom, energy or power to your "dark handlers" you have internally and externally. To break that hold on you stop allowing yourself to dissociate and stay in present time all the time doing what you choose to do. Ask for help from your soul aspects and they will help you. When you stay in the now moment or present time you are useless to your handlers and trainers.

Chapter 8
UNITY from 7th dimension ON

In the SEVENTH DIMENSION we have awareness of our soul family or the oversoul. Oversouls are created by and connected to the source's light and purity. There are an infinite number of oversouls that help direct, coordinate and organize all the incarnations of all of the creator's aspects. Each physical reality is a reflection of its particular oversoul from the plant, mineral or animal kingdom. The oversoul is the hub of the spokes in the wheel. All the aspects of the particular oversoul start with similar DNA patterns in its many life expressions and realities. Oversouls create souls and souls become humans in biology. In the 7th dimension you help guide and direct those in lower vibrations. Within an Oversoul Family there is generally harmony, balance and communication.

Each oversoul creates 12 similar aspects of itself with slightly different identities that we call soul. Each soul divides into 12 different aspects, which each divides into 12 more. Now there are 144 aspects under one oversoul and is considered a soul family. The sacred mathematics is $12 \times 12 = 144$. Each member of the family of 144 has an individual function and experiences on behalf of the oversoul. All humans have been genetically altered. We started out Lyrean and the Draco's added at least 15 to 20% reptilian DNA to the Lyreans DNA on earth. At least 12 to 20 different races from other planets added their genetics to various groups of humans on earth. None of us are pure anything any longer.

It is against Universal Law to do a walk-in of one oversoul aspect into another oversoul family. Within the same oversoul family MERGERS are frequently done or soul transfers. The oversoul my merge a higher vibrating aspect (non human) together with a human for a short time to help overcome or release a stuck pattern to further spiritual development of the human.

The EIGHTH DIMENSION or vibration is Archetypal Energy. Your essence is a prototype or template of the original version of your oversoul and the realities and vibrations it wants to experience in. This is the dimension of planets. The eighth through tenth dimensions function in terms of planets and solar systems.

In the NINTH to TWELTH DIMENSIONS there is no sense of individuality only the group expression as one "individual" planet on the 9th dimension. We are an individual solar system on the 10th dimension or a galaxy on the 12th dimension. You are primarily pure greatly expanded group consciousness.

Unity of the individual on earth is a KUNDALINI ACTIVATION that clears, balances and unifies our chakras. The energy rises up from the root chakra through all the chakras into the crown chakra and that opens our THIRD EYE. This opening is often experienced as a tickling, buzzing or pressure inside of the head or on your forehead. This activation brings new brainwaves online to allow advanced states of consciousness to integrate into your consciousness.

GAMMA brainwaves at 40 cycles per second or GAMMA RAYS are electromagnetic radiation of shorter and higher frequency wavelength than X-rays. Gamma is the strength of a magnetic field of subatomic particles. Gamma rays serve as harmonizing frequencies that store your perceptions of what you see like an object's size, color, texture, function, etc. Gamma brainwaves are thought to be associated with the brain function that creates holographic synthesis of data that is stored in various areas of the brain. These blend together into a higher perspective.

GAMMA programming by the illuminati is the secret layering in of demons. The using Gamma codes calls for demons. The ceremonies to demonize the fetus and infant occur even before they are born. Generational dark entities or demons are layered in to work with the direction of the mind-controlled slave's programming. This science deals with the occult sciences of astral projection, ESP and telepathy. SUICIDE programming is often layered into this system also. These alternate personalities would rather DIE than leave their FAMILY not blood family but the cult family. Gamma programming has Scholarship programming and rote-MEMORY skills. Gamma alters know eight different modern and ancient languages.

The EPSILON BRAINWAVES are extremely low at 0.5 cycles per second and considered to be the state yogis go into when they achieve suspended animation and/or total control of their biological functions. Hyper Gamma, Lambda and Epsilon are associated with higher states of SELF-awareness allowing conscious access to superior levels of information, insight, psychic abilities and out-of-body experiences.

EPSILON Programming done by the illuminati is a HIDDEN alter SYSTEM that may hold CIA programming, ASSASSIN programs in this or beta systems, covert, COURIER operations, learning to tail a subject, drop a tag, disguises and getting out of difficult situations. The Epsilon alter sees itself as chameleon-like and could be an animal and is color coded BROWN.

Above gamma brainwaves are Hyper Gamma brainwaves at a 100 cycles per second and Lambda brainwaves (200 cps). Then there is the extremely low Epsilon brainwaves (0.5 cps) and all three of these the Hyper Gamma, Lambda, and Epsilon are associated with higher states of SELF-awareness. These states allow conscious access to superior levels of information, insight, psychic abilities, and out-of-body experiences. Theta and Gamma brainwaves interact with the three to assist in the brain's holographic packaging of information into coherent images, thoughts, and memories. Hyper

Gamma, Lambda, and Epsilon work together. Hyper Gamma and Lambda brainwaves are fast and appear to be embedded in extremely slow Epsilon brainwaves. Slow Epsilon waves appear to be riding on the crest of the Hyper Gamma and Lambda waves. Our expanded, psychic senses are embedded or piggybacked on our five senses. The higher your vibration is the greater access to higher brain functions you have.

We went to the 3rd dimension by contracting our awareness and embracing duality the split of dark and light and a very low narrow range of vibration. We wanted to experience what it felt like to be an individual with free will and have endless choices. Morally we experienced YOU and ME separation. We created a holographic illusion SUSTAINED with our thoughts and perceptions of this reality or illusion of separation, opposites, linear time, death and forgetting. Suffering allows awareness of how it feels to go against universal law.

Our biology allowed our soul aspect to experience 3rd dimension in the "schoolroom earth" a "low dark vibration." When we vibrate or calibrate our awareness to Beta brainwaves the primary experience is 3rd dimension and below. Reality is perceived as OUTSIDE of the self and you feel you are a separate individual. The little human core belief is that it is a victim.

Honor the biology that has allowed your soul aspect to experience 3rd and 4th dimension. Now we are starting the process of expanding this illusion back into the unity we came from with the sense of individuality still in our awareness. We left the 3rd to move into the 4th dimension in 2001.

Historically when humans achieved a higher vibration or state of awareness they would ascend individually and the biology died because the vibratory rate of their consciousness was too high for the biology to accommodate. Once you expand your awareness to the 4th dimension you have memories, dreams and experiences of your parallel realities or concurrent lifetimes. In a waking state we would normally shut out our current 3rd dimension to experience other realities. The 4th dimensional biology is composed of a higher vibration of the 3rd dimensional elements. The shifts are subtle and energy shifts NOT physical shifts. 4th dimension entities have duality and their own agendas from assistance and blessing to outright interference with our development.

GAIA'S AURA the 4th Dimension

GAIA is the SOUL or consciousness of earth and is a living, sentient, breathing being just like humans and has innate intelligence. She is able to converse with all life on earth. The Order of the Arc and the House of Goddesses created the earth hologram approximately five billion years ago. Gaia is the human's support system emotionally, physically and spiritually. For the past 13 thousand years she has had a grid of dark around her and her bias was dark. In 1987 she was at neutrality.

Gaia's aura is the 4th dimension and Her emotional body. The lowest vibrational part holds all the darkness and fear that the life forms on Gaia have experienced and failed to resolve while in biology. That would include souls still addicted to substances and abuse or controlling others, the lost gray ones and earthbound ghosts that are filled with despair and hopelessness. They are STUCK in low vibrational "repetitive patterns" that feel like eternal punishment. The fear and darkness present in the lower 4th dimension creates "static" for the entire planet making it difficult for human's to receive messages from higher vibrations wanting to assist us.

Lower astral beings can and do SUCK human energy, possess humans and encourage humans to do many nasty things. Many humans are possessed and tormented by these entities that are frequently your relatives, dark aspects of you or illuminati members.

Historically Gaia released these pockets of dense energy with extreme weather like earthquakes and volcanoes. When humans help her release these dark entities the extreme weather is not needed. When dark entities or pockets of density are released into "a portal of greater light" they are not around to possess and torment the living. Releasing pockets of dark density in the lower 4th dimension means Gaia can carry more light. Humans can help increase the amount of light Gaia can carry by educating dark souls enough to move them to a portal of greater light.

The Bridge of Flowers or "PORTAL of greater light" is the point of separation from the dark near realms INTO higher TRUTHS and feelings. After death our essence can get help, guidance and assistance from humans. It is common for our dead parents to show up for more awareness and help getting to greater light. Then their vibration is high enough for angels to greet and help them adjust to the higher vibrations and impart more awareness to them. Of those trying to get to the bridge or a portal of greater light after death only 20% arrive the other 80% get lost in the near realms. Then they take another biology and lifetime to relieve their suffering. Generally they fail to increase their spiritual wisdom so the suffering continues because no higher truths have been understood and acted on.

Any human can take souls directly to the bridge of flowers so they do not get side tracked or lost in the near realms. Ask the soul if they are ready to cross and then take their hand in yours and invite any other lost souls around with them to all grab hands and cross them all at once by bringing them to the angels on the bride of flowers. Hand them off to the angels waiting. You can create a portal opening of greater light with your arms for them to enter.

Some of the rather dark ones need a little more knowledge of what is LIGHT or aligned with universal law. Share the knowledge you have ALOUD to increase their awareness sufficiently to get them to the portal of greater light. The dark ones need someone lighter to help him or her "go to the light" or "cross over" or go to the "bridge of flowers" because dark repels light.

On July 29, 2011 a small group of humans educated a legion of dark (illuminati good old boys) about how destructive their abusive parenting was to their children, spouses and grandchildren handing down those dark family practices. They were told that they did what was done to them and the way to heal it was to have COMPASSION for the abused child they were. To take responsibility of comforting and protecting the small infant and child they were. They need to embrace and protect that little one that was them. That increased their awareness enough for some of us to take them to a portal of greater light.

August 7, 2011 we worked again with Gaia to remove more pockets of density on the earth, moon and Mars. We brought a portal of greater light to move dark and dense areas into it to transmute them to higher vibrations. We started collecting density from different countries and bodies of water and life in the sea on earth. We sent the scars of wars, violence, abuse, atomic and nuclear weapons and fault lines on earth to a portal of greater light. We put a portal of light around the "illuminati force field" around earth to control and isolate us. It is being transmuted now.

We brought a portal of light into the hollow earth at both poles to release darkness in Agartha as 15% of the Agarthans are darker than light and working with the reptilians. In the crust of Gaia the illuminati have bunkers or cities and they are hiding out from the surface of earth that they have scarred and poisoned to kill many of us off with toxic food and chemtrails. By August 11, 2011 Gaia had 87% light. With more light there can be LESS extreme weather.

Because Gaia wanted the people on earth to ascend with her she asked for volunteers to experience the darkness of the past 13 thousand years we just pasted through. She knew the ones who survived would become strong enough to participate in a planetary ascension with her. The survivors incarnated and gathered together to assist Gaia. To do so you must completely release all the emotional charge of our dark experiences. The dark that made us strong must be purged to allow alignment with universal law. When you consider yourself bad or evil you have a limited range of choices before and after death. When you transition to the lower astral plane in the 4th dimension you remain there until you remember some lighter options to take. Here they will receive the darkness that they have projected out during their incarnation.   Beings of higher frequencies of your self can instruct you and assist you in any transition that you would like to create. There are Mystery Schools for spiritual training and enlightenment at the highest frequency of each sub-plane of the fourth dimension.

The "cities" in the lower astral plane would NOT be spiritual cities as the frequency is too low there instead they would experience endless illusion. These Mystery Schools can be visited during dreams or nightmares and meditations.

AKASHIC RECORDS and GRIDS

AKASHIC RECORDS are a frequency net, GRID, aura, lattice or mesh around a planet or the individual or any living thing. The grid INSTANTLY STORES the etheric patterns and DNA that encircle the planet or individual or thing. This is a detailed web of interdimensional energies that are always in motion and transition. At this time all grids internal, external and overlaying are in transition because the MAGNETICS are changing and Magnetics is the largest universal force there is. With the relocation of the earth grids from internal to the external crystalline grid around Gaia many animals have become disoriented.

There is a GRAVITY GRID in and on the surface of earth and is anchored to the spinning crystalline core of the earth. It is in the form of a dodecahedron or sphere with twelve facets. The gravity grid is rooted in the first three dimensions. The dodecahedron was the primary consciousness and geometric shape of the planet from the time of the deluge of Atlantis until the emergence of the icosahedron about 4,000 BC.

The HUMAN GRID or aura is at the level of the earth's crust extending upward as high as thirty thousand feet above sea level adjusting itself to the elevation of the planet. Human consciousness has been connected to this grid for the past 6,000 years to regulate the electromagnetic system of human DNA. It holds our memories and fears and is part of the "ley lines" and VORTEX systems or energy flows of earth.

Before 1987 there was an interdimensional cavern, the Crystal City or the Cave of Creation that kept the "record of souls" on earth. The human came and went or was born in biology and died leaving a SPIRITUAL record of the WISDOM we gained and that essence became part of Gaia's grid or aura. That is how the planet's vibration increased or decreased. The light she can carry is based on what the "human collective" has gained spiritually while on earth.

There are 2 types of akashic records An Akashic record is kept for every individual on earth, their DNA and spiritual wisdom. An Akashic record is kept for every planet and the entities that are considered an integral part of the planet. The entities or humans along with the planet itself that they "live on or in" are necessary to make a complete unified whole.

Stone circles and standing stones act like fuse boxes or acupuncture needles to receive energies from the universal grid to rebalance energy flows on earth and in individuals. PYRAMIDS and the stones from thousands of years ago were to construct a MAKESHIFT energy grid to keep the earth functioning until the Atlantean grid was reactivated and re-aligned. The moon has pyramids also.

The CRYSTALLINE GRID is a geodesic sphere of pentagons and triangles that sparkle. AFTER 1987 the human, reptilian and others collective spiritual wisdom that became part of Gaia moved from inside Gaia to the crystalline grid around Gaia. There is no longer a need to physically die to transfer information to the planet. Now our life span has become one of personal choice. Entities that live on a planet are meant to care for the planet in exchange for the planets recourses. We are slowly returning to the ancient system of balancing power and responsibility with Gaia.

The Crystalline Grid is "location specific" it contains everything that ever happened and where it happened. What we do in real time is transferred to Gaia through this grid. The grid lies upon Gaia like a blanket of awareness or energy. This is part of the collective vibrational measuring system of earth and the % of light earth carries. For the past 13 thousand years a dark fear grid has surrounded the earth from the fear we emanated but it is getting lighter. The "backup" system of akashic records for earth is stored in the whales, dolphins and AGARTHANS inside the hollow earth.

Humans that can read Akashic Records all have an individual point of perception. Their THOUGHT becomes a reality and what they think did happen, which influences their understanding of the etheric patterns. That is why there are so many DIFFERENT versions of Atlantis, Lemuria, WWII, etc. Also, there are parallel realities because each version that is put into thought is real. As grids are shaken by the solar flares repressed memories are surfacing and can create emotional chaos in us and around us.

ARCTURIAN FREQUENCY

Arcturian Group Mind and frequency is no longer in physical form because most of them do not choose to hold a body or biology. The consciousness is able to discern individual signature frequencies within the group mind and look like whatever they choose to look like. They exist in all dimensions. All the Arturians are enjoying the experience of some kind of form within some dimension of reality. Most of them experience form in a myriad of simultaneous realities as they can have multitudes of experiences within the now moment. They are not bound by time or space so nothing is too long or too far away. There are planets around the star Arcturus and some Arturians chose to enjoy the experience of living on a planet. They engage in this experience as a human would engage in a video game but they do not get lost in the experience. Most of their planetary realities are stored on the Galactic Akashic record and are not active realities.

During the fall of Atlantis some Arturians chose to incarnate on earth to help and support Gaia, she had asked for help. They agreed or contracted to stay with Gaia through the deep darkness of the last twelve to thirteen thousand years. She has made so many sacrifices for the evolution of many different races like the Draconians, Pleiadians, Sirians and humans.

Arcturians vibrate in the 7th to 12th dimension. When you raise your frequency into the fifth dimension you can experience and maintain different realities within the now moment. Arcturians as a group of beings settled originally in the constellation of Arcturus and were accepted into the Galactic Federation approximately 3.75 million years ago as The Arcturian Confederation. They are helping the earth population integrate their spiritual values with advanced technologies that are being brought on line.

Arturians provide strategic advice in transforming planetary systems and coordinating relationships with the many different extraterrestrials and aliens. Integrating global financial, political and societal systems diplomatically using conflict resolution instead of deceit and force. Arcturians have been an integral part of earth's history for eons.

Their timekeepers brought the original galactic calendar to us and later the Pleiadeans modified it. The galactic calendar is a consciousness tool used to put you in sync with the timing clock or cycles of our galaxy. The galaxy has a natural rhythm or pulse that allows life to unfold with grace. Arcturians are well known healers throughout this galaxy.

They are especially called to assist when a society is in process of making a dimensional shift. Gaia is unique in that it's accomplishing its ascension in a very short period of time along with all those living on her.

Arcturians are a horse-like mammalian closely resembling a horse. The body is muscular 7 to 8 feet tall and slender with a stylized horse's head. Skin ranges in color from a vanilla shade to a very dark brown. Arcturians possess a mane on the back of the neck and head. The hand has 4 long extremely thin flexible fingers. The eyes are much bigger than ours and pale blue or dark brown. Ears are smaller and more rounded than a horse ear.

Another group of Arcturians are 3 to 4 feet tall and generally slim with a greenish hue about their skin. They have pronounced, almond shaped eyes. They speak a tonal language that sounds similar to Chinese or Vietnamese.

Arcturians eat small quantities of food and mostly vegetables, fruits and grasses unique to their planet. They drink an effervescent liquid that nourishes them. They do not need food to sustain life they energize their body with Light. They sleep a few hours a day. They can move objects mentally. They sense telepathically and their hearing transcends their telepathy. They live approximately 1,000 years, age slowly and do not fall prey to sickness as it was eradicated long, long ago in their civilization.

Reproduction consists of a mind link of female and male energy perfectly balanced to create an energy clone. Only the wisest are allowed give birth and care for the children. They must have violet as the predominant color in their auras. The new life form is taken to a special room emanating the proper vibration until the being is ready for integration into a family unit. Many beings from Arcturus are seeded onto other planets.

ARTURIAN STARSHIPS are actually a collective being, and all components of its form are individual members of the group mind. The entire "ship" is alive or large organic sentient computers. The Arcturians create form or a pattern like the ones we sew from to create the components of their spacecraft. The "pattern" is created by their collective mind as they all join in one thought to summon the subatomic particles to collect themselves into the form of the pattern for their Spaceship. They only allow the resonance to drop to the higher fourth and fifth dimension. They do not need to use starships above the sixth dimension. They "psychically" travel through consciousness or manifest a starship if we want to make contact with others of a lower dimension. The walls provide soft natural luminescent light with no doors. You communicate tele-pathically with the wall for it to open and it accom-modates your wishes. Since the walls and floors are organic, they are self-cleaning. Arcturians glide in-stead of physically walk and they take sonic show-ers.

They travel the universe in their starships that are some of the most advanced. We have not been attacked on earth by extraterrestrial be-cause most civilizations fear the advanced Arctu-rian ships. Their spacecraft crashed on earth by ac-cident and another Arcturian group came looking for the first group and they stayed to help build the original ROMAN Empire.

Chapter 9
PORTALS are AWARENESS

When you look up to another as some kind of authority you have misunderstood and can be easily misguided. Believe in the truth found within you. When we look for answers in the 3rd dimensional Matrix we are interrupted, short-circuited and put on hold until we go within for OUR truths and knowledge.

Right or wrong are derived from your point of perception and this is a dark matrix. In reality there are only probabilities that result from the choice YOU make. Choices mean risk and an unpredictable outcome. Using your wisdom from within is a higher vibrational way to function. The higher vibrations create continuous, circular and infinite energy patterns that expand and transmute all the time. Third and fourth dimensional energy patterns have many interruptions as energy travels down the frequency range. These interruptions occur because human thought-forms of "time" create the illusion of "space" between the manifestations that light continuously creates consciously. Dark creates unconsciously.

Time and space are really ONE. Perceive these "interruptions" as portals. A portal is pure awareness. When the biology sleeps, meditates or is absorbed in a creative act pure awareness is in operation. We are all thought without our biology or the duality matrix. The Arcturian Corridor is one of many portals we pass through to change dimensions and to be born into biology on earth. We need to remain in the Matrix or Illusion until we have enough light and awareness to stop WANTING something or BE BETTER THAN someone or something in order for us to feel GOOD about the our self. Judgment and fear are the main energies that unbalance us. Inner changes are always first before our external world changes.

The higher vibrational aspects of our self know there are no laws above or outside of you. You are the law for you and the universal laws govern all. Our psyche and consciousness creates our physical reality. The human brain and DNA were imprinted with particular thought forms that affected our biology and gave us the illusion of separation and opposites. The biology is the physical dwelling place for soul aspects for a limited amount of time to experience duality and to gain spiritual awareness about darkness. Accept what you do not currently understand and wait until the understanding comes.

Motive and intent are far more important spiritually than skills and methods we have mastered to survive in the 3rd dimensional matrix. When you seriously intend to know and work with your soul aspect you will do it through any method that speaks to you. Learn to value your quiet time with your soul. In the silence you can commune and understand your soul.

PORTALS or PARALLEL UNIVERSES or time gates or doors or different realities are entrances into other frequencies. Portals have always existed on earth but are growing in size, number and dimension now. Entering a portal can give you the sensation of gentle confusion or you feel a flow or swirl of energy. A portal is created mathematically with an algorithm of interwoven energy you need to stay in the center of. There is a gauzy covering on the opening of portals to prevent lower vibrating things and entities from entering. Closed a portal looks similar to hands clasped in prayer.

Portals range in sizes from a pinhole to nine-foot in diameter. Sometimes a dot or color gets larger opening up into a portal. Going through a portal can cleanse, rebalance or expand the biology, heart, brain or consciousness. We connect to different lifetime by using a portal. There are ancient breathing portals on Gaia one is located in Sedona Arizona. The portal is always open and not controlled by dark or light.

There are portals CREATED by the population as there is in Phoenix Arizona. The more a created portal is used the longer it will stay open. Dark can highjack a light portal but then the portal may not stay open.

Who knew it takes approximately 120 years to end cycles of duality or consciousness but we are half way there now. From 1950 to 2070 is considered the end times of our personal cycle and the planetary cycle of dark and limited awareness. Moving from opposites to oneness is the BLENDING of light and dark. We are moving to universal acceptance and compassion for each other as we identify our self with our soul. The soul finds it easier to release the things the little human values highly and puts a lot of energy into. The little human struggles to survive and does "good works" or caretaking to earn a spot in heaven. That is living in survival and fear and that cycle is ending, only 60 more years.

From the spiritual or soul point of perception there isn't anything to do. When you move from the human filled with fear and control to your soul you slowly become aware that you are THOUGHT. Our "soul aspects" created opposites or contrast to understand all sides of what it is to BE dark. Most people need to go to the bottom of dark issues to explore them thoroughly before they are ready to release them. At that point they will OWN the wisdom they found and created for them self.

The wisdom you gained from darkness needs to emanate from you as an example of understanding dark ways and agendas. Even though another SEEMS to need help from your point of perception, IF they don't want your help they do not need it. Giving help or using force or power when not wanted is wasting everyone's energy and can lead you to self-doubt and disappointment. When you are emotionally involved with another it is harder to help them because they sense your need to have your beliefs confirmed. Your personal point of perception does not help others and may actually cause blocks or misdirection's for them. Whenever YOU WANT people to change you go against the universal law of allowing. They sense that because they are keen readers of your belief, intent or neediness or fear. You are not standing in your truth you are pushing an agenda.

Allowing is the knowledge that everything is as it ought to be. The universal law of ALLOWING means releasing your attachment to things and people that have chosen to hold onto their beliefs. Release your judgment, blame and attachment to PLEASING or CHANGING others and what the unconscious of the earth's population want you to do, say, be or think. Tolerance is not allowing. Allowing grants to all the same rights you want for yourself. The right to have, be and do whatever you choose as long as you avoid violating others rights or destroying our collective environment.

POWER always achieves its goals by using fear and ignorance. Ignorance opposes light and creates the illusion of separation and fear. The SOUL cannot be destroyed BUT its free and divine nature can be hidden from itself. Fear breeds the need to control and struggle for control creating the conditions for evil or dark to grow. Power creates the illusion of abundance, losing, dominating, manipulating, being the predator / victim and conditional love.

Power and dominance kill the unique qualities of those being dominated. Your reality gets stagnant because evolution is not allowed in. Power is the energy that opposes oneness because you cannot surrender to equality. By exerting power over anything or anyone you isolate and move away from unity. Power cannot truly create or destroy anything only the soul can. SOUL creates MATTER. Soul is more fanciful and adventurous than we assume. Evolution is consciousness-driven it's not accidental it is free flowing, unpredictable and joyful.

Power HIDES things, creates lies or deceptions to maintain its position.

Embracing the new and releasing of the old is considered death or end of a cycle. Some fear dying physically, emotionally and mentally but without death we become fixed in old bodies and thought forms. The transitioning happening now is to a planetary society based on mutual respect and honoring all. The hatreds and separation are no longer appropriate. Connection to our soul allows the human connection to extrasensory sources of knowledge like you're past life personalities and your acquaintances on different astral planes. There are no fixed ways to understanding your soul other than silence and knowing.

❧

The many portal opening on 11.11.11 will not be frightening as they will resonates to the mid-fourth dimension into the fifth. The "cleaning up" of the dark illuminati misdirection's is nearly complete and will be finished for the many portal openings on 11.11.11. A large group of those who were once living in the illuminati underground caves and cities have recently escaped. Once these people feel safe enough and we can tolerate the information that they want to share they will tell their stories.

11.11.11 portals will serve to awaken many who still sleep. The high frequency will amplify thoughts, emotions and abilities of those able to perceive them. On the other hand they will amplify fear and anger of those who want to retain power and control over others. There is now enough compassion to balance the fear emanating from the dark and lost ones. These events will symbolize the splitting of those who are ready to perceive the truth and those that are not.

ARCTURIAN portal or CORRIDOR

The distribution center or Arcturian Corridor or vortex or portal or stargate needs to be passed through to get from place to place in the universe. Entering the corridor allows your soul to be transported to another incarnation or planet or move out to other solar systems and other dimensions. This is a gateway through which humans pass during death and rebirth and a way station for non-physical consciousness to become accustomed to being physical.

There is an inner stargate within the Arcturian Corridor that has been in place for eons but is only opened during dimensional alignments like the one we are experiencing now. On September 9th, 2002 the inner stargate of the Arcturian Corridor was intensified and opened for all 3rd and 4th dimensional people, planets and realities to enter to start the process of increasing their vibration. Inside the corridor is a harmonic resonance and colors going from 72 in 3rd to 123 colors in the 5th dimension that activate genetic restructuring and higher vibrational skills like the ability to travel and communicate interdimensionally. The increased frequency of light expands your awareness little by little to move your essence from 3rd to 4th to 5th and even into 6th and 7th dimensions. This is happening for this quadrant of the universe.

The entire Milky Way Galaxy is increasing its frequency into a higher dimension third and fourth dimensions are becoming the fifth dimension. The fifth dimensional worlds are becoming sixth dimensional and the sixth dimensional worlds are returning to their oversouls in the seventh dimension.

As Gaia ascends, those who can match her resonance will ascend along with her. As earth returns to Galactic Consciousness the humans vibrating high enough will return to our planetary awareness. We are the planet earth partnered with Gaia and those in biology are keepers of the land and the cetaceans are keepers of the water are sworn to release attachment to 3ʳᵈ and 4ᵗʰ dimensional illusions while retaining their earth vessel.

It is most unusual for an entire planet to ascend as Gaia is doing at this time. When you adjust your vibration to Gaia you can serve as a step-down-transformer through which the 5th and 6th dimensional light can be downloaded through your body into Gaia's to assist in raising the resonant frequency of earth. In turn as Gaia's resonance rises She assists you by grounding your higher vibration to protect your biology from overload.

We enter the corridor during sleep or in a meditative state to slowly evolve, release pockets of density and raise our vibration. Clearing unconscious and conscious beliefs of limitation and feelings of separation. Transmutation of lower vibrations into higher vibrations may be sensed physically in your crown as a tingling or slight itch at the top of your head. Repetitive tasks may start to bore you or cause fatigue because part of your awareness is bi and tri locating and your brainwaves may be in theta or delta awareness. Sleep cycles may change and you need more sleep or less. The circadian cycles are shifting due to the constant stimulation of your pineal gland. Dreams and meditations are move vivid and illumined than they ever have been before. Ongoing opening of our third eye may give us sinus headaches, dizziness, colds, postnasal drip, vision problems or difficulty with concentration. Opening of your third eye increases your telepathy, empathy, intuition, clairvoyance, clairaudience and clairsentience.

PLANETS like everything in nature have LIFECY-CLES there is a limit to the planets viability before the planet needs to reinvigorate itself and Gaia is under going that now just as she has done before. Right now we are starting a medium water cycle or ice age. During the renewal process we will lose some species, which is a normal part of the renewal process. The water cycle will create weather changes. These are all natural changes in the lifecycle of a planet. A cold period starts with warming and is what some call global warming. Ice melts at the poles, but not completely.

The redistribution of cold water from the poles moves into the oceans making them raise a few inches and cool some creating larger storms than we are accustom to. The weight of the water is redistributed on the earth's crust. Where the earth is thinner or weaker you get earthquakes and volcanoes. The most powerful earthquakes will happen closest to the poles. When water temperature cools some in the ocean it will start the renewal process.

The amount of water on earth dictates the TEMPERATURE of earth. The water cycle controls our temperature and the WINDS. In water cycles there are large ice ages lasting 400-years, small 150-year ice ages and medium size water cycles like the one we are starting now. The last small ice age was in the 1200s to 1400s.

We live in cycles within cycles within cycles, loops overlapping them self of similar events. Sets of moments are points in space. Change or restructuring happens for those that can think about their thoughts or reflect on them to decide if the thought stays and you feed it your energy. Withdrawal of your thought and energy makes a belief dissolve. Embracing higher frequency thought rebalances and dissolves dark dense energy and thought.

Creation is infinite and is continuously expanding and contracting. Creation has two aspects the physical or human and spiritual or the soul that has infinite dimensions and realities. Thought, time, light and intent compose the elements of creation. Your point of PERCEPTION is creation. It is the way you individually see a thing or person or event is creation. Reality is the subset put in a dimension that is constructed by agreement with all parties involved. There is an outer flux wall around the reality within the dimension. Reality is a complex concept with many never-ending definitions. Dimensions are spheres all interacting with each other they move, swirl and shift their way our thoughts do. The different realities within the dimensions have a range of vibrations and a variety of conscious and unconscious entities in them acting out their parts or roles in any given experience.

PARALLEL REALITIES

Parallel realities are created with an individuals thought. Several individuals having similar thoughts create a group consciousness. Like-minded people gather together in awareness and in biology into small groups. The groups are psychically linked to other small groups eventually creating a huge matrix of consciousness or awareness with the same belief. This is similar to the matrix of the Internet and the way individuals connect and communicate. Joint consciousness is more powerful than the individual. Each vibrational group gets separated out and formed.

PARALLEL REALITIES arise when there are important decisions to be made so the soul aspect can experience 2 or 3 different outcomes. The soul/human chooses one experience to have and experience and then the 2nd and 3rd outcomes are experienced in parallel realities. The same issues and endings at this time on earth and during the end times of Lemuria and Atlantis are being decided and created now. OR Hitler winning WWII could be experienced. OR you married Sam instead of Kelly. OR you were a street person instead of a control freak.

There are two kinds of parallel realities VERTCAL and HORIZONTAL to give us the ability to engage in many versions or outcomes of the same experience. Vertical parallel realities exist across many different frequencies and dimensions of that version of reality. For example a person can be living now in the 3rd, 4th, 5th and 6th dimension being aware of them all and moving in and out of them. We are all experiencing the vertical flow of energy as our vibration rises. Vertical vibration flows through all the dimensions and the individual decides which one to give their attention to. At this time many are waking up in the 5th dimension and as soon as we upset our self about something we slip into the 3rd dimension.

Horizontal parallel realities exist on different levels within the same dimension. Two examples are the violent fall of Lemuria and Atlantis in the 3rd dimension and the peaceful end to the cycle of Lemuria and Atlantis that ended in the 5th dimension with the Agarthans. Each dimension has a horizontal flow that is specific to the frequency of that reality. In the third dimension, each of these parallel realities appear to be totally separate, as one of the main laws of the third dimension is the law of separation. The LAW of SEPARATION is for the 3rd and lower 4th dimension to separate awareness into small individual units. This reality was created for humans and others to understand CAUSE and AFFECT. One experience at a time was set up so that awareness of the self could be experienced as individual and sequential to train and develop spiritual wisdom through experience.

All souls start out as LIGHT.

Unbearable FEAR creates darkness, hopelessness and limited thinking. The RULES and LAWS are different for the different frequencies or realities. You can only be in a reality that you can match your resonance with. To experience the 5th dimension you must be able to maintain the 5th dimensional frequency and alignment with universal law to some degree.

The lowering of Gaia's vibration down to the 3rd dimension during Atlantis was her choice. Just as raising her frequency back to the 5th frequency at this time is her choice and the end of this cycle. We can choose to enter or leave a frequency anytime. But the close of a cycle is different. It's like the end of a movie or experience it is over and choices need to be made about where you are going after the movie. You have awareness that the cycle is ending and you focus on or start thinking about what is next for you. When you refuse to think about it and allow others to decide for you it becomes a default choice the 3rd and 4th dimension. Parallel realities of Atlantis appeared when the inhabitant's vibrations in Atlantis started dipping below the 5th dimension into the frequency of the 4th and 3rd dimension. The parallel realities of Atlantis that did not fall into fear and the 3rd dimension chose to maintain their 5th dimensional frequency by going into the "hollow inner earth" or individually they ascended into the 5th dimension into other realities or higher.

Rules of 3rd dimension are that the one or two soul aspects that follow the human losses communication with higher vibrational aspects that would let them be aware they were in an illusion of darkness with increased violence and fear. Many of us joined Gaia's birth and re-birth cycles of the last 12 thousand years and continued to get darker. During the 1940s Gaia had returned to a state of darkness corresponding to the time BEFORE the fall of Lemuria and Atlantis and she called for assistance from those in and on earth and the Galactic community. Humans assisted by their example of aligning with universal law. They refused the games of war, destruction and control. Just imagining compassion ignites our creative force and expands awareness and heals fear. Some humans are keepers of the land and some cetaceans are keepers of the water. Our planet is a personal mental creation when viewed through personal awareness and a collective creation when viewed through the group and a planetary creation through the perception of planets. Whenever we expand our awareness to another level we can perceive and experience more parallel realities.

When you change your thoughts the matrix changes. With every thought and emotion with a higher vibration we can write and rewrite our many concurrent life experiences. Change anything in any reality and all realities can change. When you change your thought patterns in one life it changes in all your concurrent expressions. From a horizontal vantage point you only see one lifetime and from a vertical vantage point you see all of your parallel lives. All our realities are interactive plays and experiences.

This power of choice has always been ours but our fears have twisted and limited our choices to imprison our awareness because we have believed the lies our handlers have told us. Just like the parent that lies to its child the child's growth is stunted in proportion to the lies the child adopts as its own.

Chapter 10
SOUL GROUPS BEING BORN

Free will and darkness are only found in lower vibrational worlds, planets or dimensions. Illusions are only found in the 3rd and lower 4th dimensional realities. Free will means the human gets to choose WHEN, how, WHY and where they want to experience their lessons. WHAT spiritual wisdom you need to gather is decided or determined before your birth on earth. You must incarnate or transfer a soul aspect into a human biology to join the earth illusion. At the exact time of our birth or when a soul transfer happens the magnetic characteristics of Gaia and you as an individual are placed in your DNA. This placement in your DNA dictates the percentage of light you will carry or your personal magnetic and electrical frequencies or the spiritual wisdom you will start out with as a human.

When Gaia was only carrying around 40% light or less the last 12 thousand years and the individual soul was darkish the child created was darkish. Add the lack of wisdom and truth that the parents carried to the darkish child and things get very challenging in a dark reality.

SOUL GROUP INCARNATIONS happen when a higher vibrating group wants to assist a lower vibrational group to increase the light they can carry.

Volunteers from the higher vibrational group come into biology at the same time as a group to create and support spiritual awareness or truths through example. During any civilization that evolved faster than the rest of earth civilizations there was a group incarnation of volunteers. For example the golden ages of the Roman Empire, Egypt and Greece had an incarnation of volunteers. Some group incarnations challenged the political, economic and religious DOGMA and darkness of the time to increase hope and awareness of universal truths.

The volunteers were NOT perfect and were subjected to the same dark pressures and fears of living on earth the rest of us need to cope with daily. Many got darker and darker like Mosses and his followers. Many of the Indigo, Crystal and Rainbow soul groups of children raised in violence and trauma here on earth have gone dark. The edge that the lighter soul group incarnations have is their higher vibration and their connection with their soul aspects that give them information and support when they asked for it. They must ask because this is a planet of free will. FEAR holds us in this dark illusion and fear leaves when you gather more knowledge and compassion for you first. Expanding to the upper 4th and 5th dimension makes it EASIER for you to discern what is illusion and what is truth.

A GROUP SOUL is the collective spiritual essence of a community, nation, or ethnic group. The group soul provides guidance and focus for the group purpose. When the group gets imbalanced it creates its own karma like the Jewish, Mormon, Catholic and Nazi groups have done. The process goes like this; individuals within the group have dark or negative purposes of force and control. Others in the group go along with it and the group gets darker and darker. The dark ones give a lie or deception and the follower's stop thinking for themselves and own the lie. Those buying the lie serve and support the dark agenda and the group gets darker and darker because those NOT buying the lie leave the group. The light ones leave to allow the dark their path and darker ones are attracted to the group and join.

The group soul is created with the birth of the group, it strengthens and weakens to reflect the direction of the group and dies when the group disbands or merges with another group. Soul groups have been arriving on earth to assist in breaking down the old and building the new with integrity, transparency and universal law. The Indigo, Crystal and Rainbow soul groups of children are here to help and arrived with self-love and self-worth. The new soul groups are confused by our self-doubt and need to please others. The children need our STABILITY and steadfastness in completing tasks. We need to model how to react to the darkness found in their families, religions and governments on earth.

Gaia was carrying around 41% light at the time of the birth of the Indigo, Crystal and Rainbow soul groups of children and each group was increasingly lighter than the group before. Indigo children had gathered their spiritual wisdom on earth. Crystal children came from other planets vibrating higher than earth and had a rough time adjusting to our darkness, lack of self-love, guilt and fear. Crystal, Rainbow and the Integrated child are from other planets like Sirius, Pleiades or the whales, dolphins and elementals.

INDIGO children were the first soul group to arrive en masse in the middle 1970s to middle 1990s. Their temperament and collective purpose was that of the warrior that challenged and destroyed old systems lacking transparency and integrity. Lacking transparency and integrity would include the family, government, educational systems, religions and all legal systems. The child or adult with the indigo vibration senses dishonesty and corruption. They know when they're being lied to, patronized, or manipulated. Indigo vibration does not understand the human emotion of guilt and feeling responsible for others "happiness" they are unable to conform to dysfunctional situations at home, socially, at work, or school. They are unable to dissociate or deny their feelings and pretend like everything is okay they know and own that it isn't. Those that resist change and value conformity will not be comfortable around Indigo energy.

Indigo children have a lot of indigo blue in their auras. This is the color of the "third eye chakra," which is an energy center inside the head located between the two eyebrows. This chakra regulates clairvoyance or the ability to see energy, visions and spirits.

CRYSTAL children were the second soul group to arrive en masse in the 1980s to 2000. Crystal children and those carrying the crystal vibration have open HEARTS and unguarded compassion they can read your thoughts and feelings. Crystal children are forgiving, modest, incredibly telepathic and have healing abilities. They appear to be fearless givers ready to understand and fulfill our needs. The dysfunctional greedy parent will wear this child out.

Before 1980s when Crystal children incarnated they hid out keeping a low profile and that made them appear meek and mild. Do not misinterpret this to mean that they are not powerful and very creative. They love touch and are very affectionate and communicate telepathically. They have delayed speech development because of their telepathic abilities they do not "need" to talk. The individual emanating Crystal energy is hypersensitive to the human emotion of fear or anger. Fear and anger is TOO low a vibration for them to process or understand. They feel the fear or anger in the hearts of others and unconsciously AMPLIFY and reflect that emotion back to the fearful or angry one. Having the fear or anger reflected back to them frequently brings out the very worst in them as they move into a survival or attack mode.

The Crystals benefited from the Indigos' trailblazing. The Crystal child follows a safer path and a more secure world. Their aura is opalescent with beautiful multi colors in pastel hues. Their eyes are large, penetrating and wise beyond their years. They lock eyes on your eyes and read your thoughts they can also see other realities and dimensions.

The Crystal individual is not similar to the autistic individual because they are among the most connected, communicative, caring and cuddly of any soul group. They are also quite philosophical and spiritually gifted with an unprecedented level of kindness and sensitivity to this world. Crystal children spontaneously hug and care for people in need. The autistic person would not be comfortable with doing that!

RAINBOW children were the third soul group to arrive en masse in the 1990s thru 2010. Rainbow children and adults with rainbow energy are fearless givers ready to fulfill our needs just as the crystal children are. Some have been raised in abusive settings creating anger and acting out in them. The Rainbow Children have never lived on this planet before and have gone to parents with crystal energy. They are an example of what our spiritual awareness can be and they demonstrate service to others. Unlike the crystal child that is laid back and patient the rainbow child has a very strong will and personality with powerful energy to exert their will. They bring harmony and balance and have very high energy with a passion to create.

Rainbow energy radiates the energy we were created with. All the colors instill health and balance in us. They are very attuned to color and its vibration. They bubble over with enthusiasm for everything in life and expect INSTANT manifestation of whatever they think about or want.

INTEGRATED or MULTIDIMENSIONAL CHILD in 2008 a few children have arrived with an even higher vibration, an INTEGRATED child. The child functions in universal round time of cycles space and aligned with universal law, not in duality. Their belief systems will come from their mental body and universal compassion. It will be difficult for them to learn and understand language the way we do because they will use pictures and telepathy. They understand and honor their connection with Gaia and nature. Their biology is more delicate than older people and they are sensitive to our pollutants and toxins just as the Crystal and Rainbow vibration are.

Then there are those of us that have been on earth forever learning spirituality the hard way. As we rise in vibration we become the ICRs special light operatives that are incorporating all the various jobs of the new soul groups and integrating them to strengthen the end of this cycle of consciousness.

These higher frequencies of light historically have always been beyond our perception. As Gaia raises her vibration, Her humans are increasingly joining the vibrations of Her plants, animals and elementals moving to the 5th dimension.

AUTISM and TELEPATHY

Autism is a complex developmental disability and neurological disorder. Social interaction and communication skills are affected. Both children and adults with autism typically have difficulty communicating verbally and interacting socially or they have little desire to communicate verbally and socially with others. Signs or symptoms of Autism begin presenting themselves at 2 to 6 years of age. The autistic individual generally relies on their telepathic skills to know the other persons thoughts and feelings. When the people in the autistic child's life are dishonesty, fearful or mean spirited those feelings can be overwhelming to the child. How well do any children process negativity and an inability for compassion in its caretakers?

Along with sensing the thoughts of the humans in the child's environment they sense the energy of those that do not have biology, the dark lost souls from the near realms. Multiple stimuli are too difficult for the autistic to process comfortably and remain calm and in control of themselves. Generally humans function in a lot of chaos not giving much attention to anyone, or thing. Most humans easily find life too stressful or painful and they are able to ignore everything by frequently dissociating. The negativity or abandonment the autistic sense from those around them with or without biology can make the child confused or fearful and they withdraw their awareness trying to change their focus by distracting themselves with repetitive stimulus. They will make repetitive noise or spin an object for hours or stare at something to block their awareness of the unpleasant things they sense. The repetitiveness helps calm them and change their focus to something they can control and feel safe with or they go to a high vibrating dimension to be nurtured.

Listening and making eye contact at the same time is a challenge for the autistic and frequently overwhelming. Autistic generally focus on one stimulus at a time, they will talk or look at you but can't do both at the same time easily. When there are too many things bombarding the autistic they shut down or sometimes lash out as a way to cope with too much or too negative stimuli. The restricted and repetitive behaviors the autistics can engage in are many times done to put themselves into a higher vibration or the 5th dimension of balance and harmony. They can access angelic beings that give unconditional love and compassion. The autistic and our pets see and communicate with other dimensions we generally deny exist because we do not see them and we have shut down our senses and feelings.

The autistic individual generally lacks the emotional attachment or dependence or codependency on other humans that we consider showing love and caring. The autistic individual needs to take care of their needs FIRST to feel physically comfortable or neurologically in harmony. Traditionally children have been forced to comply to the needs of the parent first. When you have forced yourself to conform to the customs and control of the culture you live in it is hard to adjust to a child that is compassionate to its needs for calm and harmony and standing in its own truth.

Autistic are sovereign beings and uninterested in your issues and NEED to fit in and be accepted by others. They are an excellent example of the law of allowing in action. They have no desire to fix you, enable you or take care of YOUR needs. They respect you being on your spiritual path and are mystified as to why you keep trying to force them to do things YOUR way. They sense your unhappiness and frustration with the way you do things. They are not lonely or in need of "OTHRS" approval. That is you projecting on another your feelings.

The autistic individual is not easily controlled or forced. They are indifferent to your wounded feelings. They do not judge others. They discern what gives them physical and emotional pain and try to stay away from those things and people. As a group the autistic vibrate higher than our society at large does because they are more aligned with universal law. Many of them are in communication with their soul aspects and the invisible realm. The dark low vibration of "survival truths" that we have lived with on earth is leaving incrementally or little by little. Viewing existence as fearful, depressing and feeling powerless is very limiting to our soul and not true. This illusion or earth matrix is ending.

Asperser's disorder in the autism spectrum is judged as a higher functioning individual like Dr. Temple Grandin is. She has written several books describing the thought process of the autistic. Instead of thinking verbally or with words the autistic thinks in pictures, which are easier and a clearer form of communication. All the various languages present in the world serve to prevent or distort communication and isolate groups from each other. The autistic, go through a slide show of pictures to recall information or group pictures together of similar things. Pictures are the way entities in the universe communicate just as all animals including our pets, plants, rivers, rocks and all things with consciousness communicate.

From childhood on Temple Grandin had increasing rages, anxiety and total panic attacks. Neurologically and emotionally it was painful for others to touch or hold her but she needed a way to calm herself. Frequently human touch is painful to the autistic. Partially from immature nerve endings and partially they do not understand or trust others. What you are thinking and feeling can be very scary to them. She decided to build a squeeze chute for herself. She put herself into a U-shaped sling that could squeeze her body. She could operate the sling to regulate the pressure on her body to control and relieve her anxiety. The squeeze chute she developed for herself is used in some schools for the autistic child to relieve the child from feeling out of control.

Dr. Temple Grandin has developed more humane ways to treat the animals in particular cattle by visualizing the pictures they see and what sights make them fearful and what keeps them calm. She created and developed the squeeze chute to calm down agitated and fearful cattle. The squeeze chute is a large metal apparatus that acts like a large clamp closing on the animal or person to calm them down.

CRYSTALS can be used to help the autistic screen out or step down the static or chaos they perceive and allow them to calm him or her self down.

PSYCHIC PROGRAMMING

Roughly a third of babies born on earth are born into the illuminati satanic cults and are programmed and traumatized from before birth and on. All the infants get fetal trauma programming, daytime abandonment programming, toddler programming and the steps of discipline programming. With drugging, brutality, electric shock, punishment and hypnosis infants dissociate and the core personality hides out. Most illuminati slaves do not have CONSCIOUSE awareness of any of these events. The illuminati are the generational bloodlines and the real decision makers of our governments, religions, scientists and the media on earth. They control and direct their operations covertly, which is why you haven't heard anything about them.

Some dark dysfunctional families program their babies in a less structured manner. A person in a dissociated state or fear is highly suggestible and not really present enough to help them selves or anyone else. When you keep the infant in a constant state of fear they are easy to control just as an adult would be.

10% of the illuminati children are also trained to be psychic workers and warriors for the illuminati. Usually one of their genetic parents would also do psychic reading and fighting. Toddlers at 2-3 years of age are put to work downloading information for their illuminati trainers and handlers. They psychically read other cult members and everyone else for any ANTI cult thoughts or behaviors or betrayals and report them to their handlers. They are trained to be "open to the universe" or BUTTERED all OVER the universe to receive information psychically from other planets, dimensions and extraterrestrials. The word AROUND is used as a trigger by illuminati trainer or programmer and refers to traveling to different dimensions. They mentally travel all across the universe and report what they pick up including looking for portals or tears or faults or any irregularities.

Psychic children receive information easily but are not GROUNDED anyplace. Actually the normal toddler isn't very grounded. The illuminati doesn't want them grounded or able to think for them-

selves. The psychic child has done so much remote viewing, information gathering and psychic
reading that they are in confusion about them self
and where they start and end. The psychic child
feels very fragmented and as they get older that
doesn't change. They are not able to discern their
own feelings or thoughts from another person's experiences. The adult "psychic child" has no idea
what are their issues and what are other people's
thoughts and feelings.

All children and adults blame them self when
things go wrong in their life. They think everything
is their FAULT, they feel guilty, angry and trapped.
The cult and abusive family members will reinforce
the guilty feelings and blame. Much of what they
read psychically is nasty dark abusive thoughts of
control, hate and manipulation. Illuminati psychic
children are also trained in Delta assassination programming designed to "kill psychically" those the
cult decide need killing.

The psychically programmed children and
adult are generally the ones most likely to break
their programming enough to leave the cult and
their biological family. They compulsively reach for
clarity of what is their feeling and what is another's.
Their AWARENESS and staying in present time instead of dissociation will heal them and allow their
alternate personalities to start integrating.

For EXAMPLE one psychically programmed illuminati slave was so overwhelmed by the dark insensitive cruel THOUGHTS her daily RAPISTS had she

wanted to commit suicide and tried many times in different ways when she was 4 years old. She put herself in dangerous situations like standing in front of a bull. She tried running away from home on her tricycle but needed to be home by dark. No one paid much attention to where she was at or what she did until someone wanted to use her or TRAIN her for service.

At 4 years old she split off an aspect of her traumatized self to deal with her painful existence. This four-year-old aspect dealt with any stress or frustration this woman had into her 50s. She dealt with things like any 4 year old would when they felt powerlessness, angry and upset over the many traumas and feelings of rejection and betrayal she felt, experienced and READ psychically.

At twelve years of age, she and her mother cared for her dying satanic grandpa. Grandpa's reaction was typical for an Illuminati Satanist raised with violent sexual domination, drugging, electric shock and physical control of an infant that passed for "love" in these cults. Grandpa lusted after the 12 year old. The mother of the daughter was EXCEEDINGLY jealous and felt betrayed. Mom thought SHE had earned the right to have the "love"/ lust grandpa showed the granddaughter. Mom HATED her daughter so intensely that the psychic daughter was in total distress and fear. One more reason to hate her self was more than she could process. The 12 year old made a conscious decision to stop reading minds and she crashed her programming.

When she stopped her psychic work for the illuminati she lost her value to the cult and she was almost too old to be the sexual slave she had been for the cult, the Mormon church elite and her 8 family members.

The 12 year old did maintain her psychic abilities and sensitivity with Gaia, the plants, animals, rocks and the electric fields around earth BUT NOT with the humans in her environment they were just too dark and nasty for her deal with or process any longer. She took back control of her self little by little.

Traumatized illuminati adult children are generally emotionally arrested at 2-3 years old. In this case the 4-year-old aspect that broke off worked to protect her all her adult life and she functioned emotionally as a 4 year old until in her 50s when the core personality took control of the biology and integrated the 4-year-old aspect and there were many other alters that needed integration. Seriously abused children find being an adult of any age an overwhelming challenge. Their main concern throughout childhood was surviving ONE more TRAUMA from the people they depended on for their existence, guidance and survival. There was NO TIME to develop the basic life skills. Like integrating information from your experiences, how to be functional enough to hold a job OR there is one alternate personality that is only functional at work. Their personal life is like any child without a parent.

The illuminati mothers around the world that have female children HATE them and abuse them, physically torture them and abandon them TOTALLY emotionally and frequently physically. Mom especially hates the female child because she knows the father will probably be the infant's first handler and violently rape the infant daily as training to be a child sexual slave. Mum is VERY angry at the awareness that she has lost her husbands "love" and abuse to her daughter. Male babies have similar carefully crafted experiences of abuse. Infant children are always subjected to cruel fingers, nails, teeth, cigarettes, genital torture or alligator clips, straps whips, dildos, electric shock and endless drugging.

Intimacy with another human OR staying in present time OR being compassionate with yourself are not things the illuminati adult child have experience with. The adult abused child finds it real HARD to know how to function when they are not following orders. Other people in the life of an abused child use them all the time because they are programmed to comply and always do what others want to ward off more pain. Fear of further abuse and delusions of "EARNING love" runs their life. All cult children must set aside their emotional growth and normal development because the cult or dysfunctional parent or sibling has no use for that. The child is unable to collect data from their life experiences and process the data into a workable conclusion for changes in their behavior. They are always in survival mode. Their awareness is in segments so their experiences do not have beginnings, middles and endings. Each segment stands alone. Each segment of their life is a mystery, an isolated event with not relationship to other events. They have no idea what happened before and after any event. There is amnesia from what each alternate personality does and there is generally no communication with each other.

Chapter 11
The HANDLER of HUMANS

A HANDLER is an "energy construct" that CONTROLS the fabric of a being or entity or human that has the ability to be conscious. The concept of being a handler is a neutral concept. The intent of a handler can certainly be dark or light, compassionate or violent and anything in between. Frequently handlers handle the unconscious or dissociated human or a demon possession could be considered a handler. Handlers can be another human controlling or enabling the unconscious and dissociated individual or an addiction can be handling a human. A loving supportive individual can be a handler.

Belief's' adopted from religions teachings or other doctrine the individual has been exposed to may control them and act as a handler. Someone vibrating low will distort and twist whatever they learn to serve their own personal need like some religious fanatics do and sexual addicts do. Even a dead family member or demon is an entity that has 30% to no light can possesses your biology at times to handle you. Dark entities or handlers like to help you put yourself down to lower your vibration and keep you depressed so it is easier to enter your biology and control it or use it.

The illuminati puts alters or alternate person-alities in their "mind controlled slave system" that act as internal handlers, which can be dark or light. ALONG with the internal handlers there are many human handlers and trainers to control their slaves. For example one lady had two dark inter-nal handlers that happened to be the cults idea of her mother and grandmother that taught and enforced "family loyalty" FIRST, not the blood fam-ily but the cult family. In the same woman there is a light internal handler hiding out waiting to help her. She has several human handlers and sometimes more.

The ILLUMINATI are the generational bloodlines and the real decision makers of secret societies the governments and religions on earth. They control and direct their operations covertly from the lower 4th dimension, our moon and Mars. They took or-ders from the ANUNNAKI or the mechanized world of Marduk and Draco. They have genetically engi-neered the Lyreans (humans) since the time of At-lantis and still do. They consider humans their prop-erty, chattel, and slaves or cattle to eat or destroy.

Anunnaki have advanced technology and function emotionally as the reptilian brain does with survival truths. They are not connected to the universal flow of energy and compassion. For their energy they feed from the fear they create in hu-mans. Just like a predator feeds from the fear they create in their victim.

Historically the illuminati have limited our awareness by manipulating our DNA and terrorizing us by making us believe we ARE our biology. Their goal 12 to 13 thousand years ago was to shut down our connection with our soul by destroying our telepathic powers and keeping us fearful in a LOW vibrational prison. We have perceived only the very narrow frequency range we access with our 5 physical senses under their lies and control. ANNANUKI is the new name, spelling and direction of the Anunnaki taken with the TREATY of ANCHARA in 1995 ending the galactic wars with a galactic truce of the dark (Anchara Alliance) and the light (Galactic federation). They agreed to all move to greater light in this galaxy. Anunnaki now serve the light and are using their former influence to send those still clinging to dark truths and their "ill-gotten gains" down another path. The leaders left earth in the 1990s but the underlings are still here trying to run the New World Order and the New World religious programs.

ALL illuminati infants and children are raised as Satanists with trauma based and mind control programming. The top of the illuminati pyramid consist of the 13 ruling families and each is given an area or function to fulfill. For example GLOBAL FINANCE, mind control, military or technology research and development, media, entertainment and news or religion. Number 13 is considered the highest level of knowledge. Each ruling family has a council of 13. All 13 families are shape shifters or hybrids 50%

human and 50% or more reptilian. The committee of 300 is the layers below the 13 ruling families in the hierarchy and supports the ruling families.

The INNERTERRESTRIALS are located in the earth. The clear ones in the lower 4th dimension do possess human biology at times, are demons or reptilians and psychic vampires feeding off the negative energy and fear of humans. The hybrid genetics along with trauma based programming of the infant make it easy to control those put in positions of power in politics, religions, finance and the military power. Peacekeeper Satanists give us the opposite of their name. The Carnegie Endowment for International Peace manipulates us into war all over the world and introduces dictatorships. The MEDIA selects and twists information to create fear in us.

TRAUMA BASED PROGRAMMING and MIND CONTROL was optimized and expanded during World War 2 in the Nazi concentration camps. Dr. Joseph Mengele, (Dr. Green) was the lead Programmer smuggled into the US in 1945 by the Illuminati. Formalized mind control and trauma based programming is training started as a fetus that goes through childhood and on. There are endless traumas to dissociate the human and prevent them from staying focused long enough to have their own thoughts or be in touch with their own feelings. All programming is anchored upon some type of trauma. The toddler is trained in all the sexual arts and generally becomes sexually addicted or engages in sexually compulsive behaviors as a child and adult to comfort and distract itself from the many traumas.

Instead of thinking for themselves FEAR is installed and reinforced with involuntary robotic compliance or there will be more trauma, drugging and electric shock. Trauma-based mind control was brought to us originally from Draco with the reptilians; all their children are raised with trauma-based programming. In Atlantis SLAVE BANDS were used to program 50% of the population as slaves. The band disconnected them from their soul, it was a disrupter the way a cattle prod disrupts the cattle from deciding the direction they want to go.

LEFT HANDED PATH

Those on the left handed path are considered practitioners of "black magic" or Satanists or Illuminati or the leaders of Freemasons, Mormons, KKK and the Catholic Church to name a few. The evil eye is considered to be the left eye and that is the eye you find on our money.

Some of the signs are the following. HAND on the BREAST is to show your loyalty, sympathetic attitude, submission or awareness of your lower status. HAND on NECK could mean sacrifice or the price to be paid or penalty for betrayal. CROSSED at the WRIST is binding or being bound to an oath. JOINING of HANDS signifies mystic marriage and fidelity.

CLENCHED FIST shows a threat or aggression. HAND RAISED to head shows thought, care, intellect or wisdom. RAISED HAND with the palm outward is for gratitude from extraterrestrial sources, adoration, worship, horror, amazement or when facing down to the underworld deity. ARMS RAISED with the palms of the hands facing out in a gesture of passive acceptance or surrender or have mercy or acknowledgment.

The HIDDEN HAND of the MEN of JAHBUHLUN is the hand thrust into clothing on the chest and hidden. Then the hand is drawn out again. The three reptilian composite deities of the men of Jahbuhlun are Yah (or Yahweh), Baal, and Osiris spelled all together are Yah-Baal-On. The spelling through usage became corrupted over the years to Jahbuhlun. The first three degrees of Masonry learn this sacred name of their deity and acknowledge their deity with the hidden hand.

The THREE MASONS GRIP is hands high and low and chant, "Jah-buh-lun, Jah-buh-lun, Jah-buhlun, Je-hov-ah the supreme wisdom of the serpent. The promise of the serpent made to Adam and Eve is you shall be as gods to other fellows in the Craft with serpent magic and instruct the masses on the wisdom of the serpent.

RIGHT HAND to left breast with the palm towards the breast and the fingers crooked making a type of devil's claw out of it. Drawing the hand quickly across the breast from left to right and then letting it drop to the side is the sign given by a Fellow Craft

Mason. The Fellow Craft degree is awarded in the second degree of the Order of the Illuminati. This is to remind the person of their oath and promise to keep the secrets or he should have the right breast torn open and the heart torn out.

"V" sign or two fingers upward represent the Horned God of witchcraft, often called Pan or Baphomet or the double-headed eagle the Freemasons designed. The sign of Satanism and "Gnostic Law of Opposites" are also represented in black and white checkerboard floors found in the Masonic Lodge. The doctrine of bringing order out of chaos by reconciling two opposites is what "they preach" but in practice the elite demand obedient slaves or hand across the throat.

HORNED DEVIL or El DIABLO SIGN is paying homage to Satan or it can be confused with the deaf signing of "I love you." GRIP or HANDSHAKE or "Get a grip" is a mode of recognition, unity, allegiance, bond, spiritual union, seal and devotion between Satanist or secret society brothers. They are not too impressed with females other than for reproduction, use as slaves and abuse.

Humans have given dark deities many different names; The Sun, the Central Sun, Hiram Abiff, Satan, Abaddon, Mahabone, Jahbuhlun, Saturn or Lucifer in secret religions is frequently dedicated to Saturn. Masonic authors clearly associate Saturn with Satan and the lower nature of man or the little human. "El" is the god Saturn and supreme deity represented as a black cube. All the front names and "pretend Christians" for the worship of power for the LITTLE HUMAN or ego to keep those of lower rank and the unconscious public at large hood-winked. Illuminati and Masonic theology is very similar to the Jewish Kabala. The elite believe men can become deities through reason, force, control and domination of other little humans. Like many family men do in their families. Methods used to obtain this power are deception, lies, dissociation, abuse and fear.

In the very first-degree ritual to become a Free-mason the Entered Apprentice is blindfold and a cable-tow is hung around his neck to symbolically say they are dumb or the candidate is "HOOD-WINKED." The elite intentionally set out to deceive the candidate through all the degrees up to and including the 33rd degree Freemason candidate.

The Anunnaki, illuminati and others of the An-chara Alliance believe they are doing their "gods work" by going through the universe dominating and assimilating inferior creatures and slaves, like humans are. Their god is a large white winged dragon with icy blue eyes that must be obeyed. That belief is similar to "the Christian" or "mission-aries" on earth saving the heathens or pagans to please their god and make money at the same time by taking natural resources and forcing the heathens to work for them. Americans did that to the American Indians to steal their land and de-stroy their spirituality. Not acts of compassion these are dark acts of control and force in gods name. If the reptilians are our genetic parent and handlers we have grown up just like them.

To compare and contrast dark and light, the legion of light is unconditional love and compassion for all at all times. They are multidimensional in a quantum state located everywhere. Humans have made her a single dimensional being with exaggerated human male qualities. They didn't get it right. A human becomes spiritual through their use of reason or thought and they make the very many small choices everyday that align with universal law or against universal law to give and receive only compassion.

Evil is a metaphor for the dark a human creates with their thoughts and energy. Demon possession is the result of human imbalance supported by our mythology. What we call a demon is any entity that is 70-100% dark. When one of your dead relatives possesses your biology at times they could be called a demon. Dark entities like to help you put yourself down and lower your vibration so they can enter your biology easily and take control of it. Your awareness of them and your refusal to play their dark games makes them go away to find easier prey.

॰॰॰

NO BONDING, THINKING or FEELING

People raised in generational illuminati families and that would include most all our leaders, famous people and the ones controlling world finance tend to be arrested emotionally at age 2 or 3 years in adulthood because of their childhood "training." Yes they are intelligent people especially when they do what they are trained to do but they are never allowed to bond with others, think for them self or be aware of their own feelings. On a personal emotional level "no one is home" for you to interact with and there isn't any compassion for others or the self. There may be PROGRAMMED pretend caring like Baby Talk Programming when the parent and child baby talk to each other so it appears there is a relationship and nurturing—it is only programming do not get sucked in. An illuminati child has no emotional development there is only a compliant human robot.

Fears and addictions drive there "down time." When the media covers their strange and irrational behavior it doesn't make any rational sense to us. The raping, drugging and violent out bursts seem nutty and illogical. When you consider the endless trauma, drugging, electric shock and sexual activity their childhoods are filled with their behavior starts to look very rational for them. This is NOT an excuse ONLY a reason why. A good mind controlled slave does their job to their handlers liking but when they stop doing what they are told to do and they are left with a little "free time" they ACT OUT and ACT IN with very destructive behavior to self and others. Compassion for themselves or others is not present in the illuminati and Satanists agenda. They want compliant slaves only or you can be sacrificed in a ritual.

Mind controlled slaves are always fearful with very good reason. The trainers and programmers take extraordinary measures to prevent the child and adult from bonding with anyone or anything. When you bond with someone or something you feel stronger and braver and that would reduce your fear. The illuminati feeds from the energy of fear just as any predator enjoys the fear they generate in their victims. A fearful individual is easy to control. No bonding is allowed in illuminati slaves. When you bond with another or a thing or a cause you feel stronger and are in danger of thinking for yourself. You might find fault with abusing and killing others. Being bonded to another might cause your programming to start crashing. Having an accident or feelings might start crashing your programming or old hidden memories might show up in your awareness especially with the higher vibration of Gaia. The kinds of memories you have are so strange that you KNOW you must be going crazy.

All children raised by the illuminati have POST TRAUMATIC STRESS DISORDER or PTSD. It is a severe anxiety disorder that develops after exposure to any event that results in psychological trauma. The experience overwhelms the individual's ability to cope. Diagnostically symptoms of PTSD include reexperiencing the original event as flashbacks or nightmares, avoiding things or people associated with the trauma, difficulty sleeping, hypervigilance and anger causing significant impairment in social, occupational and personal interactions.

All mind-control slaves that are full of shattered hurting alters and alternate personalities are UN-AWARE of them all collectively. Self-punishment and social withdrawal are natural symptoms of PTSD and programmed slaves. Trainers enhance the emotions of fear and anger into the alter systems because they all work to the advantage of the programs. Different alters end up holding the ANGER, fear, social withdrawal, GUILT, promiscuity and DESIRE for self inflicted punishment. Illuminati slaves are self-absorbed, judgmental, blame and criticize the self in endless loops that lead to further feelings of hopelessness and despair.

These negative and self-destructive feelings are held in check and balanced by other parts of the programming and become part of the created personalities. When the slave considers leaving the illuminati, the control systems of fear, negativity and suicide come forward to keep the slave trapped. Some alters even call or tell the handlers that the slave is trying to leave. When you DISSOCIATE you are powerless to change anything in your life. You need to be conscious to change things. When a slave or traumatized individual feels SAFE alternate personalities can and will start to integrate themselves.

During danger an intricate interaction of bio-logical, neurological and nervous system reactions occurs. This interaction causes the muscles to contract to protect the organism from harm or death. Once the danger has subsided the body is designed to SHAKE OUT excessive muscular tension. We have deadened this shaking mechanism from the iliopsoas muscles or fight / flight muscles and they are the only ones that connect the back, pelvis and legs and as they relax the natural shaking of the body reverberates throughout looking for tension and naturally dissolving it. Trauma Releasing Exercises are simple and painlessly designed to release the tension of chronic muscle contractions and there are yoga positions to provoke shaking out of our biology. Lying on your back knees bent and a bit apart to allow knees to fall out until shaking starts. http://www.consciousmedianetwork. com/members/dberceli.htm

All programming done later in life is BUILT on the initial programming all the children get around the world. AND that would be close to a third of the population. Understanding those BASIC programs laid down and the DAMAGE they do to an infants thought, psychic and emotions is the explanation for the adult's inability to function emotionally appropriately for their age. They frequently can't hold down a job for long and are sexual addicts because that is part of their training. Compulsive sexual activity is a distraction from feeling your feelings and thinking for your self.

Illuminati slaves generally have relationships with other programmed individuals so their "intimate interactions" consist of triggering each other's programs. More likely one "handles" the other. There is no real intimacy because the CORE PERSONALITY seldom makes an appearance. If you want an honest interaction you have to get the core personality to show up. That is no easy task. Even a programmed individual interacting with their child is programmed with the "baby talk program" and the child will get all the programming the parent had.

Prisoners in jail, abusive spouses, prostitutes, abused and programmed people generally have no compassion for them self or others. They are self absorbed like all dysfunctional children and adults are BECAUSE they have no awareness of their abuse as an infant and as a young child they have NO COMPASSION for them self and what that child endured. Without compassion for your abuse you repeat the cycle until you see or know what REALLY happened. That is why people marry the same type of spouse and have the same type of friends. To hopefully see the abusive pattern they are STUCK in. When the individual becomes aware of their abuse and sensory perceptions of the events the compassion for the self and healing starts to happen.

The ritually abused need to reconnect to the childhood sensory experiences they had. They DO NOT need to know each incident. Their soul aspects can give them slide shows of events and or the FEELINGS they experienced. No more pretty story cover-ups and lies. ASK out loud for your soul aspects to give you the feelings or pictures. One way or another they will get them to you. The child feels things a 100 times stronger than the adult. You need to be brave enough to stay in your biology and in present time.

One INFANT PROGRAM for ILLUMINATI slaves is The WOODPECKER GRID Programming. This programming is carried out and located in airplane hangers on military bases. The grids or little cages are just large enough for 1,000 to 3,000 human babies from ceiling to floor. They are HOT WIRED or electrified on the ceiling, bottom and sides of thee cages so the BABIES locked inside can receive horrific electric shocks. This is basic training for the illuminati. Some babies go into a fetal position and die. The others get a flash of light when a high D.C. voltage is applied. Later this flash of light is used with hypnosis to let them think they slipped into another dimension. In the Peter Pan program it is called RIDING the LIGHT. After endured the Woodpecker Grid Cages for days the infant is BRUTALLY raped.

ANAL RAPE is a training method also used by the illuminati parent on a daily basis. Raping male and female infants and children makes them go unconscious. As the child gets older and doesn't pass out you slap them so all they remember is the physical abuse. They have no conscious awareness of their daily sexual abuse. The slap is a FOCUS CHANGER to bring in a different alter that only remembers the slap and never the violent sexual assault. All 13 meridians that connect humans to their invisible aspects meet in the rectum the illuminati want to destroy that connection to keep us in fear and be easily controlled.

A MARBLE SLAB serves as an altar where black-hooded robed people take a bone-handled knife and sacrifice little children in front of the other children in the cages. Charles Manson was a programmed Monarch slave that received initial programming at China Lake and his cult was located 45 miles northwest of China Lake at the remote Myers and Barker ranches.

One location of woodpecker grids was NAVAL ORDINANCE test station / NOTS. The California INSTITUTE of Technology at Pasadena is intimately connected to China Lake's research and the Illuminati. Most of their work is for the intelligence agencies not the military. They also developed red / green color programming.

A list of major programming centers with each site's programming specialties is kept. Infants are brought into base by trains, planes and cars. The lumber mill had an agreement to secretly house the children who had their mouths tapped. Neighbors in the area were bought off and warned that if they talked they would be in trouble for broaching national security. Tied into this network was a Catholic Monastery between Sheridan and McMinnville, close to the rail network. The Union Train Station in Portland, OR has underground tunnels where children were temporarily warehoused in cages before continuing on their journey. The Jesuits were active in this part of the child procurement. Catholic adoption agencies, pregnant nuns, third world parents, and parents who will sell their children were sources of children for programming. Procuring batches of 1,000 or 2,000 children is no problem for the Illuminati working through intelligence agencies such as the CIA, NIS, DIA, FBI, and FEMA.

One child program is the WOLF, BEAR, CROW, and LION Program for illuminati slaves and was developed around 1977 in the northwest region of America. This was a twisted meaning of the "Medicine Cards" that are used like tarot cards to discover your power through the ways of the animals. The programs are based on HUNTING modules and animal characteristics and symbols. The child is shown many training films. In "training" the groups of small children they are all taught first what it feels like to be prey and then how to attack their prey or each other using mental and physical force so your prey doesn't get free or doesn't tell or INFORM on you. To compartmentalize learning and force toddlers to do things they do not want to do all illuminati programming relies heavily on drugs, electric shock and trauma. The same things are used to trigger the different stages of the programs and programming.

BEAR basic training is to build future programs on. First you are the prey and then you learn to be aware of the environment and the target. They learn to hold down the prey or each other to take what they want from the prey.

MOUNTAIN LIONS encircle, terrorize, use intricate verbal calls to intimidate and scare making easy and clean kills. They will be attacked and terrorized to the point of death by other Mountain Lion level children to make sure they understand the fear and weakness of the prey. You lead those below you by using fear, surprise, attack and terror. You climb great distances, observe your prey and report back to your Clan and trainer. As "prince of the lions" you can demand and take whatever you choose from anyone who is in your clan.

Chapter 12
SEXUAL ADDICTION / COMPULSION
Starts in CHILDHOOD

Sexual addiction or compulsive sexual activity of illuminati slaves at any age is a result of the trauma-based programming they are forced to experience. All programming is anchored upon some type of trauma and is started generally with the DAILY rape of both male and female infant done by the "trainer" generally the father. This starts as young as one week old. When they stop going unconscious and only dissociate there is more training. ALL the toddlers are trained in the sexual arts especially seduction and pleasing adults. The toddler is trained to be seductive and act like they want sex or they get more pain.

The child is trained that if they feel angry or frustrated it is their fault and they are trained to be self-abusive. The child is traumatized if they vent on or blame another for what has happened to them. Feelings of being out control, compulsive masturbation, acting out or frequent sexual activity done alone or with others is the result of being sexually stimulated and abused endlessly as a child. As adults these children use compulsive sexual activity to comfort them self and dissociate from stress or boredom or fear. Endless traumas are to make the individual dissociate and prevent them from staying focused long enough to have their own thoughts or be in touch with their own feelings or linking their thoughts to get a larger picture.

Addictions are a form of denial because the addictive activity is used instead of dealing with the unresolved issues in your life. The addiction goes away in proportion to how much compassion you have for yourself and not allowing a bully or handler to run your life will cut down on addictive escapism. Owning your experiences, doing what is best for you FIRST will cut down on addictive escapism.

ENERGETIC SEXUAL ABUSE is being seductive and treating the child as a SEXUAL OBJECT without physically touching. The interactions have a strong sexual flavor, promise or threat, flirting, and teasing masquerading as caring and acceptance. In reality it is a "set up" to manipulate the child for the predators sexual agenda. Seductive energy is very confusing to a child that is 100% dependent on an adult to exist. Sexual addiction is the most conflictual, anxiety provoking CONSUMING addiction there is.

Many scientific studies prove the hypervigilant fearful person is not able to focus long enough to access higher brain function so they generally do poorly in school and life. Because they are in survival mode they fail to move through the developmental stages most children go through and they remain emotionally and socially very immature.

Victims that are too small, weak or emotionally terrorized want to go away because they do not WANT to know what is going to happen next. They feel powerless to do anything about what will be happening to their biology that is trapped by a predator and frequently a parent. In one respect victim and predator are in agreement. The victim withdraws their consciousness and control to the predator or programmer that takes over and controls all the outcomes. When you are an infant and child disconnection helps you stay alive one more day through one more assault on your biology and your psyche. This pattern that was developed in childhood by your dysfunctional caretaker follows you into your adult life without you ever questioning YOUR practice of disconnecting from your awareness and sensory perceptions. You assume everyone does it.

When your awareness is gone so is your RESPONSIBILITY to yourself gone. What you have attracted to you have to UNDO yourself now that you are an adult. If you want to deprogram your childhood traumas or illuminati "TRAINING" and release the EMOTIONAL charge of "training" or abuse it is always best to move to the earliest incident on the chain of that particular type of event or incident. That is why remembering what happened to you as a fetus and infant is so important. It may be important to follow the chain to earlier lifetimes.

People that are recovering memories that indicate they have been programmed by the illuminati or molested often by grandpa FREQUENTLY do not go back far enough in childhood or concurrent lifetimes to release the emotional charge. When the emotional pain isn't released the human lives in their pain body or past time. They are always reexperiencing the pain when there is nothing-painful happening in present time. Going back to the earliest incident and "owning it" takes the emotional charge off of it and releases the emotion charge on all the times after the first time that particular thing happened.

This earliest programming laid in is what CREATES the dysfunctional adult that cannot function well in the greater society. The adult that is very stressed with a hair trigger and has eyes like a "deer in headlights" is suffering from their earliest abuse or programs carefully crafted for the infant to NEVER ALLOW that child or adult to think for it self or know how they feel. That individual is always in fear and obedience to "the family" and what they want. They have seen that the punishment can include death. Some traumas or forms of torture for the illuminati infant and toddler during their TRAINING may be; confinement in boxes, cages, coffins or animal carcasses. Being restraint; with ropes, chains, cuffs, near-drowning and extremes of heat and cold, including submersion in ice water, and burning chemicals. They are subjected to spinning, hanging upside down and in painful positions, endless electric shock and drugging. Slaves are forced to ingest body fluids like blood; urine, feces, flesh and go hungry and thirsty, eating disorders are common. Frequent sleep deprivation and sensory deprivation to create disorientation along with endless drugging to create illusion, confusion, and amnesia, Ingestion or intravenous injection of toxic chemicals to create pain or illness, including chemotherapy agents and limbs pulled or dislocated. Snakes, ants, spiders, maggots, rats are use to bite the slave and induce fear.

Parents of the infant or toddler also act as trainers and create near-death experiences like asphyxiation by choking or drowning, with immediate resuscitation so the parent or trainer appears to be their savior. There is forced participation in child pornography and prostitution, infants are raped and killed. Part of the training allows possession by dead relatives and demons that are allowed to control the biology as ALL the illuminati are Satanists.

Victims of trauma-based programming and mind control have odd reactions to benign stimuli that trigger them. TRIGGERS or FOCUS CHANGES can be words, ACTIONS, behaviors, SEEING a particular thing, a particular smell, sound, message or phone call and some get psychically contacted. Ask your soul aspects, which trigger you need to be conscious of the MOST. Ask if they will help you notice it when it happens? Many popular movies, jingles and songs have triggers in them. For example, a stare into eyes or a punch in stomach is a CUE to be submissive. Some noises or car noises are a CUE to be fearful. When they see an apple or hear a police or fire siren they know "they are being watched." Hick-up can be a cue to go into CONFUSION. Lady in Red is a trigger song to get undressed.

Oh those eyes or you have beautiful eyes, you are so beautiful, he is so sexy are triggers to make the slave feel safe, trusting, loved and sexually excited. "You like it wild." You are a Wildcat, Tiger, and little girl, Bitch, Kiss me. Tiger is a trigger to go mentally foggy or into a state of hypnosis and act like a robot. Kissing is a focus change to make you forget what happened just before the kiss. Pain works well to change focus, pain in the head and stomach. SOME triggers start a series of actions. A SLAP is a trigger to close down the receiver program, to SHUT the file and open another program. They make repetitive, robotic statements that do not make sense in the context they are in. "I want to go home" means they need to report to their trainers. Compulsively sung songs are used to trigger programs. Dissociative and neurobiological responses to trauma prevent experiences from being processed into our normal memory.

The VICTIM program is used to make the slave feel they have lost a love when all that has happened is handlers were switched. Stories you tell yourself are YOU programming yourself. Sexual behavior or lust programs can be started or intensified with a bite on the ear, a whisper of demeaning remarks in the ear or prolonged kisses. You where beaten after the sexual abuse to forget what was really going on, all you remember is the physical abuse or the focus change. A nurturing program is baby talk back and forth to your children and they baby talk back but no intimacy or caretaking is really felt.

MIND CONTROL is when you allow others like parents, schools, religions or your country to do your thinking for you and you robotically follow their directions. Microchips are no longer needed to program the population because the powerbrokers are using telepathy and satellites to electronically augment their two-way communication with ELF, VLF and LF waves making you think their messages are coming from within your own brain or mind.

PERSONAL GREED and SPIRITUAL DEBT

The world and individual DEFAULTS of 2006 through 2008 were all about the little humans personal greed individually and collectively. The top of the illuminati has studied and knows the human well. YES the Illuminati orchestrated the "easy money" or credit without much likelihood of being paid back to further their agenda of a "one world economy" that they could have total control of and consequently control of the population on earth. The Illuminati goal was to destabilize world finance by encouraging the individual person and the few people that controlled finances in each country to indulge their GREEINESS. Humans being as dark as most are bought into the illusion of getting something for nothing. Like the animal you trap in a cage by putting in some food they like not realizing they gave up their freedom for the bait. DEBT is disregarding the truth of your finances and borrowing from the future. Not ethical behavior for the individual or the group.

Creating debt individually and as a country is trying to fill the empty spot we have internally. We feel we are OWED something from some source outside of the self. The lack of acceptance and love we feel INSIDE us is a result of not having compassion for the self. By rejecting, judging, belittling the self and refusing to love our self FIRST we have created our own personal SPIRITUAL DEBT that needs to be paid to us. We try filling the empty spot with THINGS money can buy. In many families and consequently in many adults, money is given INSTEAD of love and acceptance. When the child is not nurtured and accepted for the fact that it exists they look externally for validation and support. You can pay others to pretend they care about you or buy things for yourself to prove you have value. But having or spending money lacks the internal acceptance and the peace that comes from the ethical behavior and communion with soul that the human craves. All the money and things in the world cannot make you accept YOU and feel compassionate toward you. That is something only you can do for you, it happens internally.

The spiritual definition for ABUNDANCE is NOUR-ISHMENT for each day, one day at a time in the now moment. Abundance or wealth is you having compassion for the self and alignment with universal law. Limited, unconscious and unable to love the self, people are fearful, angry and stuck in survival, poverty or lack. They will often dominate, trick or manipulate those with less money and more fear to keep them in fear and survival. Misery loves company and so does darkness so it can feed off of your energy. The victims fear and suffering feeds the hungry predators need to feel powerful. That is why you pull the bugs legs off one at a time instead of just stepping on the bug killing it.

The illuminati BANKERS offered easy money with subprime loans hidden in them. The financial people in each country except for Germany could not resist the illusion of getting something for nothing. And that was thinking that trickled down to the people in each country. In 2002 the illuminati fueled what appeared to be economic growth with their subprime loan scams. Subprime is less than top quality and the loans were made to borrowers with poor credit ratings and no way to pay back the loan. A smart salesman from Merrill Lynch sold the German bank IKB Deutsche Industriebank Americas "triple A rated bonds." These were complex bond funds to prevent buyers from noticing they contained subprime mortgages. Historically Americans have been trusted.

When the kid defaults on the loan the parent pays. When banks crash the debt goes to the government and the government is the taxes the people pay. The people have taken on the debt of the subprime LOANS they helped inflate by borrowing more than they could repay. From 2002 to 2008 states increased their debt just like the citizens increased their personal debt. 2 to 3 times MORE DEBT was created with easy money around the world than was ever true before. The increased debt resulted in underfunded pension plans and MORE future debt. A larger percentage of pension money was invested in risky assets that failed. Public employees increased their salaries with no revenue to meet the salaries.

The government pushed their debt onto the states by not funding programs like education and health care. States pushed their debt onto the city governments by not funding programs. Worldwide debt went from $84 trillion to $195 trillion. By 2008 the subprime mortgage bond market had collapsed from mortgage delinquencies and foreclosures happening around the world.

In Ireland debt is 24 times greater than its annual tax revenues are. Spain and France debt is 10 times its annual tax revenues. Icelanders wanted to stop fishing and became investment bankers. Cheap credit between 2002 and 2007 and subprime loans made the 3 banks of Iceland fail. Iceland has become a hedge fund since it went bust in October 2008. In Greece the state or the government borrowed money from the banks to pay their debts. The Greek government stole or squandered the money they borrowed from the banks and didn't repay their debt because Greeks fail to pay their taxes. Greece has become a ward of other countries willing to give it money.

The BACKUP PLAN devised in 1944 to prevent the financial disaster we have created with the illuminati and our personal greed was a United Nations specialized agency. In "pre second world war" under Bretton Woods of the United Nations was designed to stabilize unstable exchange rates and devalued economies to prevent a monetary crisis in any country. This agency evolved into the IMF. The International Monetary Fund is a global organization made up of 185 countries to oversee global financial health and provide assistance when needed to its country members.

Today the IMF goals are "to promote international monetary cooperation, exchange stability and lend money to developing nations. Members from each country help govern the IMF.

Criticism of the IMF is that they are illuminati operated and controlled and their agenda is to control all financial matters globally and create a one world currency that will in turn control all the people on earth.

Americas system for financial balance is the FEDERAL RESERVE BANK that works through central banks to regulate and control the money supply for America. The Federal Reserve Board implements the policies of the Federal Reserve Bank that is PRIVATELY OWNED by Illuminati members and has NEVER been AUDITED since the day it was formed. Money is moved and counted with BOOKKEEPING entries because the funds have no gold or silver backing them. The Federal Reserve Bill was pushed through Congress in the last few days before Christmas of 1913. This Act established the most gigantic TRUST and Central Bank on earth. We have no idea what is in the trust and no control over it.

The lack of ethics and integrity the individual functions with is reflected in the groups and national behavior of its country. Michael Lewis in his book BOOMERANG, 2011 has written with clarity and in detail about individuals in their countries and how they handled their money and who conned whom. Some of this information I got from his book.

A few investors in 2006 bet against the subprime mortgage bond market with a hedge fund. A hedge fund is a private, actively managed investment fund using high-risk methods like investing with borrowed money. Hedge fund managers got very rich.

Germany controls the financial fate of European countries. Their bankers bought subprime bonds for the German people and are considered criminals. The German traders made no money personally unlike the traders in America who are very wealthy criminals.

August 5, 2011 for the first time our credit rating was lowered and the American government is less likely than ever before to repay its debts.

POVERTY of the soul is what we need to consider. The human is temporary and it is the humans reaction to what they experience that creates the illusion of lack or poverty. Limited, dark or unconscious humans tend to be fearful and stuck in survival, poverty or lack. They think they are ONLY biology and do not carry much light.

The universal principle of MONEY is that it is an artificially created symbol used as a substitute for stored or borrowed energies earned, spent, owed, claimed or exchanged. To have value the symbol must be acceptable to the others in a society.

The universal principle of POVERTY is that you are "in poverty" to the degree that you withhold your productivity or energy in hope that someone else will offer his or her energy instead. Then you have unfairly claimed the energies of another and squandered them by forcing others to do what you have not done for yourself.

Poverty comes to those fixated on penny pinching or excesses of trash or hoarding because such a narrow focus is imbalanced and creates lost friends, poor health and lost opportunities. Focus on any ONE thing at any cost is always imbalance.

Poverty comes to you when you are productive and FAIL to properly take hold of your reward (energy) in a suitable manner. Those convinced that they are unworthy or incapable of having anything of value will be in poverty as self-love is lacking. Lasting joy and wealth come from WITHIN you.

CANDIDA has a SPIRITUAL SIDE

CANDIDA yeast the parasitic fungus that causes thrush, serious complication in AIDS patients, is found in or causes cancer, and is a chronic concern for many women. Candida is Latin for clear and white, the whiteness of milky quartz not chalk. Candida has become a MUCH larger problem in humans than our soul aspects figured it would be. Yeast was designed to CLEANSE and get rid of the unwanted. The way the fish, carp cleanse their environment in the fish bowl or lake. When the biology has an excess of Candida it forms a white cloud between the human and their soul aspects greatly distorting awareness and communication. A 30% INCREASE of Candida yeast is happening now, obesity and diabetes keep increasing also.

The cloud that yeast creates in your thoughts spiritually represents you withholding nurturing and compassion from the self and what your biology needs to function at its peak. Contact with the soul gives the peace we crave. Eating more sugar and processed food doesn't give the peace going within offers. When there is an excess of Candida you have forgotten to take care of yourself FIRST and stand in your truth. Spiritually you may release things and people too rapidly OR cling to them when they need releasing. Throat and coughing problems might be a failure to stand in your truth to the people in your life.

Dr. Tullio Simoncini says cancer is a FUNGAL INFECTION. Fungi BLUNT the immune system and then invade an entire organism. Eventually the tissue gets exhausted and produces only undifferentiated cells. A cancer could be considered a SOLID ABSCESS where the yeast colonies form a hard center with host cellular reaction all around it. Anti-fungal drugs are INEFFECTIVE in treating tumors because the solid colonies are attacked only on the surface. After the first administrations of drugs yeast become resistant. Simple fungal infections can LAST FOREVER and for MANY lifetimes.

Sodium BICARBONATE is what Dr. Tullio Simoncini and other doctors have identified as uniquely able to penetrate the Candida yeast systemic infections: for cancer, AIDS and many other diseases of the internal organs. The best substance to eliminate skin cancer is iodine tincture, particularly when it is spread onto the growth. Sodium bicarbonate is the main ingredient in baking soda but not the same as baking soda, because that has other ingredients. Candida does not adapt to sodium bicarbonate the way it does to anti fungal drugs. The patient is given sodium bicarbonate orally and through internal means like an endoscope. Without surgery the sodium bicarbonate is placed directly on the cancer or fungus. Some real late stage cancer can take months to cure but in others, like breast cancer where the tumor is easily accessible it can only take days to leave.

Chapter 13
UNIVERSAL LAWS and PRINCIPLES

Universal laws are generated from the legion of light's ONLY law "Give and receive only unconditional love and compassion." That is how we can keep our individual and personal universe balanced and harmonious. The universal PRINCIPLES are derived from universal law and are the fundamental truths, found within the universal laws. Principles are morally correct attitudes or general scientific theorem or law having many special applications across a wide number of fields.

The Ten Commandments are the Universal Laws simplified as "rules" to point out what is a dark or light choice. Self-love happens internally never externally. Those that believe self-love happens externally and not internally will always "covet" or yearn to possess, not allowing others their freedom. Those that worship external "authority" give away their energy, power, thinking and frequently their biology and health.

External results of an action are not significant. The inner character growth or decay that develops in you during a challenging struggle is what matters. Aligning with the laws assures a positive outcome eventually even while living on this dark planet. Going against the laws creates suffering to strongly point out there are other options of greater balance and harmony for you to consider.

The source or creators are a partnership and not a singular entity. They are light-beings that are primarily consciousness in a quantum state or the smallest unit of anything physical. They do not judge or force anything or anyone they emanate unconditional love at all times. The legion of light is the Intelligence behind all creation that exists only in present time. We experience different realities in different dimensions to increase our own spiritual understanding of what is light. The physical world and our struggles with matter, biology and dark truths are temporary challenges or educational tools and learning experiences.

Connected closest to the legion of light's purity and clarity are oversouls and they create souls. Each soul starts out with 5 aspects and a new aspect gets added to the original 5 aspects as they go through challenging experiences in a reality or matrix to increase their spiritual truths and wisdom. The soul aspects incarnate into biology after gathering 15 to 20 more aspects to experience darkness. The higher self or 2 to 4 other soul aspects follow the human's vibration or their level of compassion to stay connected to the human. All soul aspects are androgynous and the other soul aspects are the "think tank" lining up synchronicities to enrich the human experience and enhance spiritual wisdom. The soul aspects can and do make their presence known through our sensory perceptions.

DARK SOUL ASPECTS the rules of the earth experience are that 2 to 4 soul aspects are to help and support the human. When the little human lowers their vibration as a result making many dark choices the soul aspects get pressured into following the little human into the lower vibrational bands and thought patterns making all a darker gray. When a human holds the frequency of war, vengeance, and anger or hate that becomes the frequency the human emanates and attracts to the self.

When you emanate or project a vibration of fear you are NOT being FORCED to do anything. You have become the CREATOR or catalyst for anger, vengeance and violence. When you ADOPT the belief or obsession of a reality another created for you it becomes your truth and what you emanate. Do you emanate victimhood, trickery or self-hate a family member has introduced you to and you adopted as your own?

When the human asks their soul "What do you think of me?" and the response is negative or belittling that is a soul aspect that is confused, ignorant and dark. Only a dark soul aspect will tell you that you are stupid, ugly, and evil, not worthy or encourage the human in abusive behaviors. You can ask for a 100% light aspect to answer your questions. A soul aspect that carries light is always honest but never negative. Any answers you get that are negative, dark or confusing ignore because that comes from a wounded entity without compassion. If you have created dark soul aspects the human needs to take responsibility for uncreating the darkness.

ACTION, ALLOWING and ATTRACTION

The universal law of **ACTION** means the human must ACT first to start the ball rolling. Make the many little moves to get things started and prove your commitment to the direction you are moving in. Then your soul aspects will line up synchronicities for you in the vibration or level of compassion you function in.

The universal principle of **INERTIA** is a body at rest remains at rest until an equal and opposite reaction happens moving the body at rest into another direction or vibration or reality or dimension.

The principle of **LEVERAGE** is a small amount of energy exerted in present time is used to change the course of future and past events. A change in your awareness NOW will change your future and past experiences. The future or past is never fixed in the timeless loops of multidimensions we exist in.

Allowing is the knowledge that everything is as it ought to be.

The universal law of **ALLOWING** means releasing attachment to YOUR need for others to be the way you want them to be. Stop trying to please or change others and release your judgment, blame and attachment to what the dark ones want you to do, say, be or think. Tolerance is not allowing. Allowing grants to all the same rights you want for yourself. The right to have, be and do whatever you choose as long as you avoid violating others rights or destroying our collective environment.

Prayer is giving your power away and asking another to do what you need to do for the self. A good soldier or follower needs a good leader. Being the follower or leader goes against universal law. Each of us must create and focus on our own thoughts, awareness and reality. Force and saving others is you trying to force your reality on others. That helps none and keeps you in a low vibration and darkness.

The universal principle of **COMPENSATION** is that we receive "like energy" to the energy we emanate in our thought and action. Our invisible soul aspects and "not the little human" decide how and when we are compensated. The reward is as large as you are able to NOTICE and receive graciously. Limitation comes from your refusal to see, own and use the wisdom or clue offered to you. Synchronicities, "gods gifts" or the legion of lights blessings need to be allowed in or received by YOU.

In the 3rd dimension we operate with the "dark rules of survival" and staying alive. We have been raised, taught, used and controlled by dark truths. Religion and darkness have been dismal failures at teaching people to love themselves. When you don't love yourself FIRST your ability to love anything or anyone else is drastically reduced and you fail to accept your high vibrational gifts and awareness.

The universal principle of **LIABILITY** says we are held liable for the use, abuse or neglect of the rights we have and earned.

The universal principle of **PROSPERITY** is you prosper in direct proportion to the enjoyment you receive in seeing the prosperity of yourself and others. Your prosperity is denied in direct proportion to your feeling of guilt, envy or hostility for being prosperous or witnessing other's prosperity. When one prospers all may prosper. Maintain a prosperous attitude even in states of poverty to move to prosperous states.

The universal principle of **AWARENESS** is that you NEED to observe the illusion of separation that duality presents and realizes how many dark truths there are on earth. This reality is a role-playing game designed to increase your discernment and spiritual wisdom about the way dark behaves and the truths the dark holds and live by. Ascension is out of the question when you fail to love yourself first.

The universal principle of **RELATIVITY** is viewing and understanding from a particular viewpoint and that is relative and accurate to the viewer's point of perception.

The universal law of **ATTRACTION** reflects with clarity and truth the dark or light beliefs you hold and operate with. Conscious or unconsciously our vibration emanates from us attracting more of what we broadcast. The human is a temporary vehicle working with a soul aspect to think and create their beliefs into material form so they can experience what the logical consequence of their belief leads to.

It is like seeing your reflection in a mirror. When we are angry, vengeful, withdrawn or have compassion and emanate love we get more of what we emanate. Blaming your soul, god or your friend drives YOUR vibration down, darker and away from your biggest supporters. It is imperative to own your creations even if you created with some very dark gray energy. Never judge yourself or others discern if there is a more balanced direction to take your energy.

The universal principle of **ACTUALITY** is that a thought or belief is real and does not need to exist in material or dimensional form.

The universal principle of the **UNCONSCIOUS MIND** or **BRAIN** is that it is unable to distinguish FACT from FICTION and follows what it is told. If convinced a piece of ice is red hot it will experience a burn. If convinced you are a failure it will make sure that you fail. If it receives conflicting data it produces conflicting results.

ENTRAINMENT, BALANCE and COMPASSION

Our dark thoughts and going against universal law started a great many life times ago. There have been many dark lifetimes of codependency or being the victim and predator for those on earth. To change or evolve out of those patterns of dark the human needs to take the lead and break the dark contracts by telling your dark soul aspects "no more." There are many dark soul-to-soul agreements or entrainments you are probably still honoring and triggering that hold you in a band of darkness.

The universal law of **ENTRAINMENT** requires that two vibrations existing in the same space MUST adjust and combine to have a single resonance. For Example, on a scale of 1-10 if one is at 3 and the other is at 7 they are required to both be at 5 ish. Or if one is overpowering it will pull the other to their level so both would move to 3,4 or 6,7.   The universal principle of **Reconciliation** allows different qualities to get unified into similarities to diminish differences and decrease conflict.

BALANCE

The balance of practical and spiritual energy raises your vibration. Our DNA is now able to go beyond the restrictions placed there by ages of dark energy and our inactivity.

The universal law of **BALANCE** is to maintain order and harmony within the divine universe. All choose to exist and when they are in synchronicity with other entities and events balance is maintained.

The universal principle of **HARMONY and AGREEMENT** says efforts to manipulate, trick, coerce or force harmony and agreement will only DISRUPT previously established areas of harmony and agreement. Between the most hostile enemies the smallest area of harmony and agreement can be discovered and increased. Any compromise with any force divides or harms instead of unifying. Harmony may be found in conflict when that is essential for the welfare of all. INNER peace nourishes external harmony.

The universal law of **MACROCOSM** and **MICROCOSM** is the first law of infinity. The whole of a complex structure is represented more or less in all of its parts. A drop of water has what the ocean has.

The universal law of **CORRESPONDENCE** is "As above, so below." The laws of physics explaining the physical world of energy, light, vibration, and motion have their corresponding principles in the etheric world.

The universal law of **CAUSE and EFFECT** or **RECIPROCAL action**, nothing happens by chance or outside of universal laws. The fact that you cannot identify them is irrelevant. For every action there is a reaction or consequence some place. You get back what you give. Its not personal it is physics.

The universal principle of **PARADOX** recognizes the movement of energies in four dimensions simultaneously. Cause and Effect, Inertia, Microcosm and Macrocosm and Vibration come together in a collision at a certain point. Paradox seen on a flat plane is like a stone dropped in a stream with the ripples moving out. Paradox in a CUBED space would create VIBRATIONS in all directions. Paradox touches high levels of vibration and dense levels of vibration SIMUTANIOUSLY and the entire area appears to be alive. Whatever is said about one level holds true or is untrue for all levels.

The universal law of **COMPASSION or DIVINE ONENESS** is that everything is created from universal energy, which is unconditional love and connection to everything.

The universal law of **FREE WILL** is divine will granting each entity the right to direct and pursue his or her life so long as he or she does not violate the same right of others. A right that excludes the rights of others is NOT DIVINE.

The universal principle of **GRACE** is a divine being can apply mercy to set aside karma.

The universal law of **DIVINE MANIFESTATION** is win-win-win-win to benefit all involved and harm to none. Any harm to another in the process or outcome of manifestation is not DIVINE and carries karmic debt.

The universal principle of **FREEDOM** is space for expansion and growth for ALL without restricting others space to grow. No one is free until each is free and all free each other.

The universal principle of **EXPANSION or INCLUSION** is never-ending as long as there is more to be included in the definition or description. We are all that THERE IS and all that can possibly be. Moving from expansion to exclusion or contraction you describe something as LESS and that limits you. When you are this and not that you limit you.

TRANSMUTATION and RESPONSIBILITY

The universal law of **PERPETUAL TRANSMUTATION of ENERGY** is that all humans have the power to change the conditions in their life. Raising your vibration is hard work needing you to stay in your biology and focus your thoughts. We all have the skill set to do that. The imbalances you attracted to you have to be UNDONE by you.

The universal principle of **ENTHUSIASM** is that new thoughts make you feel enthusiastic. A new belief always shows up to challenge an old one. This repeated action increases enthusiasm. Stagnating in old patterns and relationships makes us become robotic with lost enthusiasm for life. The lack of personal and spiritual growth depletes our energy and light disconnecting us from our soul aspects.

The universal principle of **JOY and INNER PEACE** increases with deeper connection of the little human to their soul aspects giving up the human free will for living in divine will.

The universal principle of **HAPPINESS** is how you feel about WHO you are, what you do, and what you have that creates happiness. Not who you are, what you do, or have.

With all freedoms and increased awareness there are responsibilities to create win-win-win for all involved.

The universal principle of **RESPONSIBILITY** is when you have the ability to respond to the needs of others you receive energy from all those you respond to. This is not stealing energy but creating energy together synergistically.

The universal principle of **AUTHORITY** is the one aware, worthy and capable of accepting the responsibility for an act has the authority to act, initiate and accept responsibility for the act. Many want authority but will not take the responsibility for their action.

The universal principle of **PENETRATION** is anything that is seen with great attention and quality of awareness penetrates the heart, which emanates into all of consciousness.

The universal principle of **PRIVACY** every person is entitled to the right of individual privacy we can't infringe, read minds or question their motives without their consent.

The universal principle of **SILENCE** when the little human views experience through the souls point of perception you can experience chaos with nonresistant and silence.

The universal principle of **SECURITY** you can express in a manner that allows your best performance without infringing on the expression of others that have the same right.

POVERTY and PROJECTION

Poverty of the soul is the consideration. The human is temporary and it is the humans reaction to what they experience that creates the illusion of lack or poverty. Limited, dark or unconscious humans tend to be fearful and stuck in survival, poverty or lack. They think they are ONLY biology and do not carry much light.

The universal principle of **MONEY** is an artificially created symbol used as a substitute for stored or borrowed energies earned, spent, owed, claimed or exchanged. To have value the symbol must be acceptable to the others in a society.

The universal principle of **POVERTY** is that you are "in poverty" to the degree you withhold your productivity or energy in hope that someone else will offer his or her energy instead. You have unfairly claimed the energies of another and squandered

226

them by forcing others to do what you have not done for yourself.

Poverty comes to those fixated on penny pinching or excesses of trash or hoarding because such a narrow focus is imbalanced and creates lost friends, poor health and lost opportunities. Focus on ONE thing at any cost is imbalance.

Poverty comes to you when you are productive and FAIL to properly take hold of your reward (energy) in a suitable manner. Those convinced that they are unworthy or incapable of having anything of value will be in poverty as self-love is lacking. Joy and wealth come from WITHIN you.

The universal principle of **PROJECTION** is that you created your STORY with your thoughts. Your reality is YOU projecting your thoughts into this reality or matrix or dimension. Any reality is constructed by agreement with all parties involved to determine the controlling matrix or grid system in a given reality. Reality is a complex concept with many never-ending definitions. Your stories can only be changed or rewritten from within you by changing your thoughts in the now moment. Those wishing to see joyful experiences instead of reruns, trash, and violence must refuse to allow such things to fill them.

The universal principle of **REALITY** is a measurable thing like an idea, object, event or person that can be seen, heard, felt, and then this object has reality or mass.

The universal principle of **THOUGHT** is that energy follows your THOUGHT. Seek or wonder about something and your thought will take you there. You need to discern what is true or valuable for you in what you find.

The universal principle of **VIBRATION** is that everything in the universe, physical or NOT moves in waves or circular patterns and has a unique vibration, color and sound. That applies to all our sensory perceptions, feelings and thoughts.

Chapter 14.
CONCEPTS to INCORPORATE

These are concepts to incorporate and always work on while raising your vibration. As with the universal laws and principles there is no particular order that anything needs to be done in.

1. Relate to all others without blame, judgment or drama.
2. Know the little human or ego or soul aspect is experiencing duality in cooperation with the biology in a reality of darkness to build their spiritual wisdom and understanding about dark truths.
3. Knowing comes first and then there is action and creating.
4. Connect and continually commune with your soul aspects. Stand in your belief's loud and proud. Fall into harmony with your biology and soul aspect to align with universal law.
7. Trust yourself and what you know inside.
8. Love yourself unconditionally first.

LEVELS of COMPASSION

Compassion or love or light or awareness goes from zero to a 100%. Your soul always has these percentages about everything available for you all you need to do is ask out loud for them. Unconditional love is 100% light. Unconditional love is what we were created from. Individuals and groups carry all carry percentages of light that can change easily.

The vibration and light on earth are slowly increasing making it difficult for the unconscious to stay that way. The increased light and awareness coming from the sun and photon belt are helping many people on earth awaken to the spiritual aspect of them self. Those not wanting to awaken are experiencing more pain and suffering and are acting out. Some are releasing their biology. This is a planet of free will.

UNCONSCIOUS or NEGATIVE

The lowest vibrating emotions and sensory awareness are UNCONSCIOUS or NEGATIVE. The little human's capacity for **compassion** and the amount of **light** their vibration carries correlate to each other.

Around 70 to 60% of the earth's population is unconscious or negative or dark. They are slow vibrating, self-hating, numb, apathetic and dissociated. They act dead or operate in self-pity, blaming others and the self. They have vengeful thoughts and are angry, antagonistic, addicted.

To deal with their suffering they shut off their feelings and senses. Humans and Bellatricians or reptilians have been stuck in this vibration for millennia. We have been playing in the victim predator cycle leading to more of the same. We lived on the planet that reflected the groups dark thought and behavior.

In experiencing contrast the human made many dark, self-destructive choices and become very WOUNDED, guilty and fearful. Finding your way back to the light and alignment with universal law again may well be a challenge. The HUMAN needs to reeducate the self and is responsible for reeducating the GRAY higher self and soul aspects.

Level Below 0 to zero carries **no light to 15% light.** They act dead and operate in self-pity, blame, addictions and using other entities, humans and animals. They are easily possessed by any entity and the most likely possession is a dark ancestor or relative. The feelings and emotions of the little human that is unconscious include denial or numbness or dissociation. You would need to work yourself UP to level zero and RESENTMENT, anger, antagonism, blaming, acting out, SELF-hate and living life in anxiety and fear.

Level 0 carries is **15 to 30% light.** They operate by abandoning their biology and their awareness. They feel betrayed by their biology and life. To cope they shut off their feelings, emotions and sensory awareness are unconscious and unaware.

Our biology is a vehicle and learning tool used to have dark experiences. As we got increasingly darker we got attached to doing what would keep our biology alive. We became physically and emotionally attached to stuff or people that could keep the biology safe and satisfied. Most behaviors in the "earth illusion" are about maintaining the biology physically.

Historically only about 10% of the dark individuals had fully functional light bodies and the ability to organize and focus the other 90% unconscious ones. Dark is extremely tenacious, wounded, angry and committed to their creator Anchara that ruthlessly went after total conquest of the galaxy. Just as the abused child will protect and hang onto his or her abuser. They reason that is all they have going for them.

The dark were great angry warriors that lacked the skills and "creative energy" needed to build and maintain an empire or much of anything else for that matter. They were good for short bursts of destruction like the military is trained for and gangs and criminals prepare for. Building, creating, nurturing and support take self-love and self-worth the dark does not have.

The largest areas of seduction for darkness are SEXUAL and / OR the belief that another human can KNOW more than they know. When you decide to follow another because you fear them or think they have greater spiritual wisdom or trickery that is not higher-level truth. The practice of following or fearing others translates into WORSHIPPING a false god or idol instead of loving and having compassion for YOU first. Dark choices and illusional power can be very seductive, addictive and intoxicating for the little human unaware of the infinite essence in the finite vehicle of its biology.

We have allowed the government to drug and dumb down our children and adults with their toxic food and chemtrails. We provide the labor and are the natural resource for the secret BLACK government we have.

HALF CONSCIOUS

When you reach for higher thoughts little by little you go in and out of awareness and are a HALF CONSCIOUS human functioning emotionally in fear, indifference and boredom. You would need to work yourself UP to antagonism, anger contentment, hopefulness, and CONSCIOUSLY create some.

Around 30 to 40% of earth's population is **HALF CONSCIOUS** as they go in and out of awareness. They function in fear, indifference or boredom. They operate by being oppositional, angry or in pain. They are self-absorbed and dramatic, gossipy, frequently leave their biology and live in past time. They are limited by their fears and irrational beliefs. They twist facts to defend their reality. Having curiosity is moving in the right direction.

Frequently they believe they are better than you or THEIR group is better than YOUR group so they can force you to do things their way. They can blame you and gossip about you to make you feel worthless. Adults enjoy doing that to a child. Blame allows you to AVOID taking responsibility for YOU. In their families, religions and other institutions they experience fear, pain, punishment or rejection. They allow bullies and leaders to do their thinking for them surrendering their personal thought and freedom. When you stop thinking for yourself you are powerless, robotic and predictable as most humans are. The vast majority of our society is unconsciously programmed to fit in and not make waves. Venting or leaving your trance or dissociated state long enough to express rage or anger is not thinking that is reacting.

Level 1 carries **30 to 50% light.** They operate by being oppositional, angry, in pain and HATING. They are self absorbed, gossipy, fearful and frequently leaving their biology or living in past time. They are limited by their beliefs and fears and are irrational much of the time with a rather limited vision. They twist facts to defend their half conscious reality.

Level 2 carries **50 to 60% light.** They operate by being conventional, traditional and cautious they are 3/ 4 CONSCIOUS. They upset themselves when others do not follow the rules and are very proud of that. They DO tend to squelch the enthusiasm and inventiveness of others. They are followers, not adventurers and want to be entertained. They are cautious and want to be average, fit in.

Level 3 carries **60 to 70% light.** They are thriving, inquisitive, seeking and mostly conscious. At 60% and higher we are able to start loving and having compassion for our self. They function in awareness, interest, eagerness and creativity.

Level 4 carries **70 to 80% light.** They are eager, cheerful and enthusiastic. To move to the top of this band you would need to work yourself UP to JOY and passion as you merge with your soul. Consciousness determines your DESTINY not technology. With 70% light an entity or demon cannot posses your biology because you won't let it

Someone that can carry more light than dark emanates some grayish light because there is always a hidden agenda with the light so it is not pure. They start showing compassion for the SELF. They can tap into the "universal sources of information" them self without an entity as a go between like a guide, angel, ascended master, alien or your higher self. There are no secrets in lighter vibrations. Everyone has access to everything.

You are now aware that you have never been a victim and created victim experiences to increase your understanding of darkness. The dark presents endless moral dilemmas to mold, develop and create our moral character and choices. The legion of light imposed quarantine on earth roughly 12,500 years ago when Atlantis sank and the earth plunged into darkness. We have experienced frustration, misery and pain to let us know we needed to make different choices. As their light and awareness increases they thrive, are inquisitive, eager and creative.

FULLY CONSCIOUS

The fully conscious human reach's for higher vibrational thoughts and works on getting in sync with their soul aspects and universal law. 2 to 4% of the population is fully conscious. Carrying 70% light or more an entity or demon cannot posses your biology because you won't let it. Functioning steadily at 80% light you are vibrating high enough for your soul to enter the space around your biology and you are passionate as "the little human" starts to merge with their soul aspect. At 80% light or more you have had your half dark / half light ascension. At 80% light you are joyful and enthusiastic. You have committed to being compassionate with your self and your biology.

Your guides, angels, higher self and imaginary friends say good-by one way or another but you need to notice them leave. You are not being abandoned but you will feel lonely. The old falls apart and there is a time lag until the new kicks in or gets down loaded. Have faith during the time lag as you are in the void and at zero point energy. It is wise to release and grieve for what you were and what you experienced.

Individuals working on ASCENDING are about 1% or less. For those wanting to merge with their soul or higher self and ascend they need to bring their compassion, vibration, light or awareness up to 80% so you are vibrating high enough to allow your higher self / soul to reside in your auric field.

Level 5 carries **80 to 90% light** and is called **IN and OUT** because 50% or less of the little human has merged with their higher self.

Level 6 carries **90 to 95% light** and is called **BAL-ANCING** your biology and DNA. The human needs to show gratitude daily toward their biology for all its service to your essence. Be grateful to the biology for all the abuse you have experienced especially in childhood and managed to stay alive and functioning because of its innate intelligence and willingness to work with you in this density. The re-connecting of your strands of DNA into loops and your biology transforming from carbon base to crystalline base. Your immune system has worked by fighting invaders now the THYMUS absorbs and transmute invaders. Your higher self changes the codes and the biology changes accordingly. The little human only needs to allow and NOTICE the changes. You have now merged 80% of the little human with your higher self and you are functioning as soul more than like the little human.

Level 7 carries **95 to 100% light** and is called **SOARING** the little human emotions, drama and concerns are mostly a thing of the past BUT your biology is still in the 4th dimension and needs to be lovingly cared for. The little human contribution is to be present in their biology awake and aware in present time. You are 90% melded with your soul. Before moving to level 8 you MARRY your higher self / SOUL.

Level 8 carries **ONENESS** and infinity the human functioning as one unit with the higher self or soul and you are out of duality spiritually, mentally and emotionally. Your biology is a vehicle from earth. The loneliness is gone now.

Level 9 is the **COMPLETION** of an era, a cycle, or level for you personally and it is not physical death or loss of your biology. It is the silence of completion.

ABOUT YOU

Your auric bodies hold your entire story along with everyone else's story and your soul aspects read it all. They are happy to share it WHEN you are ready to hear it. Just ask them. They are waiting for you to find them inside of you and commune with them and remember your wisdom. Ask one question at a time and allow the answer to come to you even if it needs to come in a dream.

The FULL knowledge of what actually happened to you and your reaction to what happened will heal your programming, addictions, self-destructive patterns and the dark choices and seductive illusional power the little human thinks it has. Are you aware you are an infinite essence in a finite vehicle of biology? Putting a pretty story on your childhood experiences and concurrent lives to please or deny will not change a thing and it never has. Keep clinging to your pretty story and you will stay stuck.

Humans generally carry or fall in sync with the beliefs and behaviors of their family, relatives and the people they "hang out with." When you are looking for higher or lower truths than your current ones you need to ACTIVELY get involved and focused to change.

240

What I write is not for fun it is slow reading and slower understanding. This is a DOING project for the individual and their soul aspects. This is not a group project for fun and distraction.

About Me

I have been an educational therapist for the past few decades and have done private therapy with children, adults and families. I understand how devastating CHILD abuse is and how it will negatively impact a person of any age in any number of concurrent lifetimes. For the past 40 years I have taught emotionally challenged and severely learning disabled students and adults from grades 3-12 in public schools as well as in my own private school, these experiences have showed me what works and what does not work so well.

The "cause and effect" of things have always fascinated me and I always want to "know more" so I studied the field of psychology and sociology my entire existence and many more lifetimes than just this one. The illuminati programmed have showed up at my door and I wanted to help the ones that wanted to break free so I have studied and researched even more about the way the illuminati program all their children and how to crash the programming.

Inside you KNOW

Bonnie

CERTIFICATIONS as an Educational Therapists (AET), Principal, Special Educator of Emotionally Disabled and Learning Disabled, Reading Specialist, Art Instructor and Supervisor

EXPERIENCE Spiritual Therapist, Acting Principal, Program Director and Community Coordinator for the Severely Emotionally Disabled, grades 7-12 Designed, developed and implemented a therapeutic approach. Collaborated with psychologists, peace officers, parents and Administrators. Have designed, developed and implemented curriculum, for at-risk, multicultural students in inner cities. Facilitated group processing. Helped to transition students into the mainstream, Student advocate for student's and families rights. Peace Officer for Harris County Texas, Member of the Biltmore Who's Who

www.ingramcontent.com/pod-product-compliance
Lightning Source LLC
Chambersburg PA
CBHW032059280526
45784CB00012B/150